Day 8
Converting

W9-BZA-103

Name: _____

Score:

Problems 1-15: *Find the answer for each blank space.*

Problem #	Fraction	Decimal	Percent
①	3	_____	300%
②	$\frac{1}{25}$	0.04	_____
③	$\frac{3}{25}$	_____	12%
④	$\frac{1}{50}$	0.02	_____
⑤	$\frac{3}{50}$	_____	6%
⑥	$\frac{41}{50}$	0.82	_____
⑦	_____	0.75	75%
⑧	_____	0.2	20%
⑨	_____	0.25	25%
⑩	_____	0.125	12.5%
⑪	_____	$0.33\overline{3}$	$33.\overline{3}\%$
⑫	_____	$0.66\overline{6}$	$66.\overline{6}\%$
⑬	_____	0.1	10%
⑭	_____	0.7	70%
⑮	_____	0.01	1%

© Libro Studio LLC 2020

¼ % 5.3 ✗ 3.107 290 = 8 ∧

Name: _____

Score:

Problems 1-4: *Shade the circle with the equivalent decimal.*

27%	84%	10.6%	1.2%
1. Ⓐ 27	2. Ⓐ 0.084	3. Ⓐ 1.06	4. Ⓐ 12
Ⓑ 2.7	Ⓑ 0.84	Ⓑ 0.16	Ⓑ 1.2
Ⓒ 0.27	Ⓒ 8.4	Ⓒ 0.106	Ⓒ 0.12
Ⓓ 0.027	Ⓓ 84	Ⓓ 0.016	Ⓓ 0.012

Problems 5-8: *Shade the circle with the equivalent percentage.*

$\frac{7}{25}$	$\frac{9}{50}$	$\frac{1}{2}$	$\frac{3}{5}$
5. Ⓐ 12%	6. Ⓐ 90%	7. Ⓐ 20%	8. Ⓐ 30%
Ⓑ 25%	Ⓑ 18%	Ⓑ 2%	Ⓑ 15%
Ⓒ 70%	Ⓒ 45%	Ⓒ 10%	Ⓒ 12%
Ⓓ 28%	Ⓓ 9%	Ⓓ 50%	Ⓓ 60%

Problems 9-20: *Find the equivalent decimals and percentages.*

9. 0.6% = _____

10. _____% = 3.7

11. 500% = _____

12. _____% = 0.009

13. 2% = _____

14. _____% = 0.13

15. 17.8% = _____

16. _____% = 0.628

17. 64% = _____

18. _____% = 4.05

19. 20.3% = _____

20. _____% = 1.347

© Libro Studio LLC 2020

Name: _____

Score:

Problems 1-10: *Match the equivalent numbers.*

1. $\frac{1}{2}$ = F

2. $\frac{1}{20}$ = I

3. $\frac{3}{4}$ = E

4. $\frac{59}{100}$ = B

5. $\frac{2}{10}$ = J

6. $\frac{2}{5}$ = A

7. $\frac{11}{20}$ = D

8. $\frac{29}{1000}$ = H

9. $\frac{1}{3}$ = G

10. $\frac{9}{25}$ = C

Ⓐ 40%

Ⓑ 59%

Ⓒ 36%

Ⓓ 55%

Ⓔ 75%

Ⓕ 50%

Ⓖ 33.$\overline{3}$%

Ⓗ 2.9%

Ⓘ 5%

Ⓙ 20%

Problems 11-14: *Shade the circle with the equivalent decimal.*

35%

11. Ⓐ 3.5
    Ⓑ 0.35
    Ⓒ 35
    Ⓓ 0.035

10%

12. Ⓐ 1
    Ⓑ 0.001
    Ⓒ 0.1
    Ⓓ 0.01

6%

13. Ⓐ 0.06
    Ⓑ 60
    Ⓒ 0.6
    Ⓓ 6

42%

14. Ⓐ 4.2
    Ⓑ 0.42
    Ⓒ 420
    Ⓓ 0.042

© Libro Studio LLC 2020

Name: _____

Score:

Problems 1-15: *Find the answer for each blank space.*

Problem #	Fraction	Decimal	Percent
①	$\frac{23}{100}$	_____	23%
②	_____	0.75	75%
③	_____	0.15	15%
④	$\frac{2}{3}$	$0.66\overline{6}$	_____
⑤	_____	0.05	5%
⑥	$\frac{2}{4}$	0.50	_____
⑦	$\frac{1}{25}$	_____	4%
⑧	$\frac{1}{2}$	0.50	_____
⑨	$\frac{1}{3}$	_____	$33.\overline{3}\%$
⑩	$\frac{3}{5}$	_____	60%
⑪	_____	0.8	80%
⑫	$\frac{1}{8}$	0.125	_____
⑬	$\frac{1}{4}$	_____	25%
⑭	_____	0.20	20%
⑮	$\frac{1}{50}$	_____	2%

© Libro Studio LLC 2020

Name: _____

Score:

Problems 1-4: *Shade the circle with the equivalent decimal.*

77%	**20.5%**	**112%**	**0.4%**
1. Ⓐ 0.77	2. Ⓐ 2.5	3. Ⓐ 11.2	4. Ⓐ 0.04
Ⓑ 7.7	Ⓑ 0.025	Ⓑ 0.112	Ⓑ 0.004
Ⓒ 0.077	Ⓒ 2.05	Ⓒ 1.12	Ⓒ 0.4
Ⓓ 77	Ⓓ 0.205	Ⓓ 112	Ⓓ 4

Problems 5-8: *Shade the circle with the equivalent percentage.*

$\frac{3}{5}$	$\frac{2}{4}$	$\frac{12}{25}$	$\frac{7}{50}$
5. Ⓐ 15%	6. Ⓐ 20%	7. Ⓐ 48%	8. Ⓐ 14%
Ⓑ 25%	Ⓑ 50%	Ⓑ 12%	Ⓑ 7%
Ⓒ 50%	Ⓒ 40%	Ⓒ 24%	Ⓒ 28%
Ⓓ 60%	Ⓓ 25%	Ⓓ 36%	Ⓓ 70%

Problems 9-20: *Find the equivalent decimals and percentages.*

9. 54% = _____

10. _____% = 0.007

11. 12.1% = _____

12. _____% = 0.085

13. 137% = _____

14. _____% = 6.12

15. 2.2% = _____

16. _____% = 0.953

17. 45.9% = _____

18. _____% = 0.3

19. 0.3% = _____

20. _____% = 1.5

© Libro Studio LLC 2020

Name: _____

Score:

Problems 1-10: *Match the equivalent numbers.*

1. $\dfrac{4}{5}$ = ___B___

2. $\dfrac{9}{20}$ = _____

3. $\dfrac{1}{2}$ = _____

4. $\dfrac{11}{25}$ = _____

5. $\dfrac{2}{3}$ = _____

6. $\dfrac{3}{4}$ = _____

7. $\dfrac{97}{100}$ = _____

8. $\dfrac{4}{10}$ = _____

9. $\dfrac{2}{5}$ = _____

10. $\dfrac{13}{1000}$ = _____

Ⓐ 44%

Ⓑ 80%

Ⓒ 50%

Ⓓ 97%

Ⓔ 25%

Ⓕ 45%

Ⓖ 1.3%

Ⓗ 75%

Ⓘ 40%

Ⓙ $66.\overline{6}\%$

Problems 11-14: *Shade the circle with the equivalent decimal.*

0.8%

11. Ⓐ 0.08
    Ⓑ 0.008
    Ⓒ 8
    Ⓓ 0.8

470%

12. Ⓐ 0.47
    Ⓑ 4.7
    Ⓒ 47
    Ⓓ 470

5.1%

13. Ⓐ 0.51
    Ⓑ 5.1
    Ⓒ 0.0051
    Ⓓ 0.051

19%

14. Ⓐ 0.19
    Ⓑ 19
    Ⓒ 1.9
    Ⓓ 0.019

© Libro Studio LLC 2020

Name: _____

Score:

Problems 1-15: *Find the answer for each blank space.*

Problem #	Fraction	Decimal	Percent
①	$\frac{1}{5}$	0.2	_____
②	$\frac{1}{20}$	0.05	_____
③	$\frac{1}{3}$	_____	$33.\overline{3}\%$
④	_____	0.01	1%
⑤	$\frac{1}{4}$	_____	25%
⑥	_____	0.15	15%
⑦	_____	0.75	75%
⑧	$\frac{1}{2}$	0.50	_____
⑨	_____	$0.66\overline{6}$	$66.\overline{6}\%$
⑩	$\frac{23}{25}$	_____	92%
⑪	_____	0.1	10%
⑫	$\frac{1}{8}$	0.125	_____
⑬	$\frac{1}{10}$	_____	10%
⑭	$\frac{1}{1000}$	0.001	_____
⑮	$\frac{17}{50}$	_____	34%

© Libro Studio LLC 2020

Name: _____

Score:

Steps:		1. Line up the decimals and add place holders	2. Solve like a normal addition or subtraction problem.	3. Move the decimal point down.
Example 1: Addition	0.79 + 6.5	0.79 + 6.50	1 0.79 + 6.50 7 29	1 0.79 + 6.50 7.29
Example 2: Subtraction	13.8 − 5.18	13.80 − 5.18	12 7 10 13.80 − 5.18 8 62	12 7 10 13.80 − 5.18 8.62

① 0.57 + 45.8   ② 8.57 + 3.71   ③ 2.7 + 4.4   ④ 91 + 8.78

⑤ 7.5 + 12.66   ⑥ 0.89 + 0.75   ⑦ 53.1 + 27.4   ⑧ 0.3 + 1.071

⑨ 8.74 − 1.29   ⑩ 2.03 − 0.6   ⑪ 20 − 6.781   ⑫ 63.6 − 4.9

⑬ 53 − 0.356   ⑭ 7.6 − 7.21   ⑮ 1.6 − 0.3   ⑯ 0.91 − 0.62

© Libro Studio LLC 2020

Name: _____

Score:

① 3.1 + 7.18   ② 4.2 + 7.1   ③ 4.87 + 3.3   ④ 1.52 + 9.18

⑤ 1.1 + 8.18   ⑥ 4.17 + 1.12   ⑦ 35.7 + 4.72   ⑧ 5.7 + 5.33

⑨ 62.2 + 4.63   ⑩ 8.58 + 9   ⑪ 9.33 + 4.1   ⑫ 7.22 + 2.43

⑬ 8.11 − 2.2   ⑭ 2.33 − 1.11   ⑮ 73.9 − 1.33   ⑯ 6.55 − 5.77

⑰ 12 − 4.32   ⑱ 1.99 − 1.68   ⑲ 3.22 − 1.11   ⑳ 6.88 − 4

㉑ 9.37 − 4.70   ㉒ 3.51 − 2   ㉓ 11.6 − 4.21   ㉔ 6.22 − 3.81

© Libro Studio LLC 2020

Day 17
Adding and Subtracting

Name: _____

Score:

① 13.4 + 1.47

② 1.27 + 4.9

③ 2.23 + 3.73

④ 81.3 + 4.44

⑤ 1.5 + 3.22

⑥ 4.71 + 1.32

⑦ 3.53 + 8.26

⑧ 22.5 + 3.79

⑨ 4.23 + 7.91

⑩ 1.11 + 15.3

⑪ 6.56 + 7

⑫ 1.55 + 7.74

⑬ 65.99 − 0.72

⑭ 9.42 − 2.12

⑮ 7.14 − 3.43

⑯ 5.12 − 2.12

⑰ 5.20 − 3.11

⑱ 7.12 − 3.44

⑲ 8.44 − 1.99

⑳ 5.00 − 4.00

㉑ 6.11 − 6.01

㉒ 8.55 − 2.77

㉓ 10 − 7.72

㉔ 9.22 − 2.18

© Libro Studio LLC 2020

Name: _____

Score:

① 6.2 + 0.43

② 3.12 + 1.12

③ 1.13 + 9.18

④ 7.44 + 3.12

⑤ 7.22 + 1.66

⑥ 9.03 + 5.5

⑦ 32.6 + 2

⑧ 3.72 + 10.5

⑨ 82.4 + 0.08

⑩ 3.71 + 1.8

⑪ 7.7 + 6.4

⑫ 6.5 + 75.3

⑬ 0.72 – 0.59

⑭ 29.5 – 2.13

⑮ 8.12 – 1.88

⑯ 64.3 – 23. 4

⑰ 1.2 – 0.98

⑱ 5.51 – 2.7

⑲ 3 – 2.28

⑳ 18.2 – 0.06

㉑ 9.12 – 6.05

㉒ 10 – 5.99

㉓ 6.14 – 5.62

㉔ 4.26 – 4.18

© Libro Studio LLC 2020

Name: _____

Score:

① 7.43 + 4.2

② 53 + 8.09

③ 2.16 + 6.66

④ 7.20 + 0.00

⑤ 0.22 + 1.23

⑥ 6.53 + 0.94

⑦ 15.81 + 2.63

⑧ 5.29 + 0.53

⑨ 8.5 + 5.21

⑩ 0.07 + 2.55

⑪ 2.99 + 3.23

⑫ 8.23 + 1.95

⑬ 9.53 – 9.18

⑭ 12.5 – 5.12

⑮ 7.08 – 1.28

⑯ 2.52 – 2.18

⑰ 5.71 – 4.23

⑱ 8.32 – 0.75

⑲ 50 – 2.23

⑳ 9.27 – 8.28

㉑ 9.32 – 9.28

㉒ 4.27 – 4.00

㉓ 2.23 – 2.22

㉔ 38.23 – 12.9

© Libro Studio LLC 2020

Day 20
Adding and Subtracting

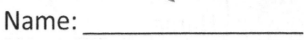

Name: _____

Score: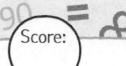

① 6.39 + 8.07

② 79 + 3.12

③ 3.17 + 1.28

④ 0.29 + 3.22

⑤ 8.12 + 3.11

⑥ 7.27 + 2.14

⑦ 11.2 + 2.18

⑧ 8.27 + 1.23

⑨ 3.89 + 0.15

⑩ 7.37 + 8.48

⑪ 3.82 + 3.09

⑫ 2.23 + 26

⑬ 13.7 − 3.23

⑭ 9.32 − 8.31

⑮ 5.52 − 2.35

⑯ 6.13 − 0.22

⑰ 4.31 − 3.32

⑱ 7.22 − 3.24

⑲ 15 − 2.21

⑳ 10.6 − 10.43

㉑ 3.27 − 2.00

㉒ 0.63 − 0.06

㉓ 12.04 − 9.5

㉔ 9.27 − 3.27

© Libro Studio LLC 2020

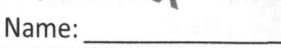
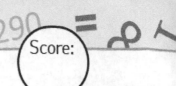

Name: _____

Score:

① 5.4 + 4.48

② 7.27 + 4.2

③ 1.12 + 1.18

④ 41.2 + 7.94

⑤ 0.38 + 2.72

⑥ 8.12 + 5.19

⑦ 1.28 + 8.13

⑧ 7.17 + 10.9

⑨ 0.04 + 2.38

⑩ 35.5 + 3.72

⑪ 1.99 + 2.32

⑫ 17.88 + 2.68

⑬ 9.22 − 9.06

⑭ 38.6 − 4.87

⑮ 3.53 − 3.28

⑯ 7.8 − 3.84

⑰ 7.45 − 2.86

⑱ 7.16 − 4.8

⑲ 4.25 − 2.56

⑳ 9 − 8.48

㉑ 5.28 − 2.98

㉒ 9.74 − 0.66

㉓ 40.2 − 5.34

㉔ 9.47 − 7.74

© Libro Studio LLC 2020

Name: _____

Score:

① 4.01 + 15.3

② 0.65 + 7.25

③ 53.1 + 3.83

④ 4.19 + 6.7

⑤ 3.73 + 5.2

⑥ 8.3 + 6.25

⑦ 10.22 + 8.43

⑧ 8.24 + 9.73

⑨ 6.39 + 6.07

⑩ 0.41 + 3.73

⑪ 64.2 + 4.29

⑫ 8.8 + 6.93

⑬ 8.24 − 2.5

⑭ 5.52 − 5.25

⑮ 17.01 − 7.05

⑯ 8.87 − 8.08

⑰ 7.98 − 4.32

⑱ 6.12 − 3.04

⑲ 8.54 − 4.8

⑳ 8.5 − 4.63

㉑ 11 − 3.34

㉒ 3.47 − 1.09

㉓ 3.47 − 3.04

㉔ 6.37 − 3.43

© Libro Studio LLC 2020

Name: _____

Score:

① 7.2 + 1.67

② 8.17 + 5.14

③ 3.27 + 5.18

④ 3.37 + 2.11

⑤ 61.4 + 3.17

⑥ 9.52 + 30.8

⑦ 0.67 + 8.11

⑧ 5.1 + 2.19

⑨ 6.85 + 2

⑩ 2.7 + 5.19

⑪ 1.79 + 1.56

⑫ 22.2 + 7.61

⑬ 2.8 − 1.22

⑭ 6.35 − 0.9

⑮ 13.26 − 6.12

⑯ 9.96 − 9.21

⑰ 5.57 − 4

⑱ 6.51 − 3.24

⑲ 8.91 − 8.84

⑳ 7.43 − 5.11

㉑ 5.1 − 1.78

㉒ 4.5 − 4.14

㉓ 12.05 − 2.10

㉔ 5.17 − 4.21

© Libro Studio LLC 2020

Name: _____

Score:

① 0.07 + 6.73

② 7.12 + 5.90

③ 9.23 + 9.12

④ 8.12 + 3.91

⑤ 9.12 + 9.9

⑥ 4.3 + 6.21

⑦ 4.13 + 6.12

⑧ 3.2 + 9.21

⑨ 4.33 + 3.12

⑩ 7.6 + 6.18

⑪ 8.33 + 2.99

⑫ 3.1 + 5.31

⑬ 4.71 – 3.03

⑭ 5.73 – 1.23

⑮ 7.47 – 3.55

⑯ 6.3 – 5.53

⑰ 7.13 – 2.2

⑱ 8.32 – 3.26

⑲ 7.8 – 4.64

⑳ 9.34 – 9.18

㉑ 5.23 – 3.23

㉒ 5.34 – 3.99

㉓ 9.42 – 4.59

㉔ 8.34 – 7.32

© Libro Studio LLC 2020

Day 25
Adding and Subtracting

Name: _____

Score: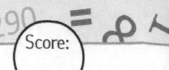

① 7.8 + 9.15

② 6.04 + 1.53

③ 7.31 + 8.92

④ 9.9 + 12.54

⑤ 6.7 + 0.81

⑥ 1.72 + 5.61

⑦ 7.42 + 5.23

⑧ 9.43 + 2.78

⑨ 7.7 + 5.01

⑩ 0.35 + 0.76

⑪ 74.3 + 15.9

⑫ 1.18 + 16.5

⑬ 3.23 − 1.17

⑭ 8.27 − 1.72

⑮ 10.04 − 3.78

⑯ 9.47 − 0.18

⑰ 6.46 − 4.94

⑱ 3.53 − 2.43

⑲ 9.43 − 4.56

⑳ 6.47 − 6.35

㉑ 9.34 − 6.8

㉒ 7.3 − 2.39

㉓ 11 − 3.92

㉔ 0.88 − 0.59

© Libro Studio LLC 2020

Name: _____

Score:

① 3.12 + 8.35

② 3.62 + 6.2

③ 9.23 + 21.4

④ 1.32 + 6.21

⑤ 2.29 + 5.13

⑥ 1.3 + 10.45

⑦ 7.16 + 2.39

⑧ 0.08 + 14.7

⑨ 3.36 + 0.8

⑩ 9.32 + 4.1

⑪ 47.3 + 28.18

⑫ 8.1 + 9.4

⑬ 7.17 − 2.21

⑭ 1.21 − 1.21

⑮ 5 − 3.12

⑯ 7.42 − 5.18

⑰ 71.3 − 45.7

⑱ 3.07 − 0.72

⑲ 50 − 23.61

⑳ 1.1 − 0.84

㉑ 5.36 − 2.3

㉒ 8.7 − 1.78

㉓ 3.52 − 3.08

㉔ 6.47 − 0.5

© Libro Studio LLC 2020

Name: _____

Score: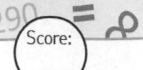

① 48.7 + 5.72

② 3.5 + 3.17

③ 7.1 + 2.96

④ 0.39 + 3.17

⑤ 7.21 + 9.34

⑥ 4.06 + 9.8

⑦ 4.24 + 6.3

⑧ 9.52 + 73.3

⑨ 8.84 + 35.7

⑩ 0.38 + 0.48

⑪ 5.37 + 9.32

⑫ 2.3 + 4.5

⑬ 5.99 − 0.78

⑭ 9.2 − 2.12

⑮ 5.7 − 3.43

⑯ 12.5 − 2.12

⑰ 84.2 − 3.11

⑱ 4.04 − 3.86

⑲ 4.92 − 1.99

⑳ 10 − 1.07

㉑ 6.11 − 0.61

㉒ 5.06 − 2.77

㉓ 7.92 − 7.72

㉔ 6 − 2.18

© Libro Studio LLC 2020

Name: _____

Score:

① 7.1 + 7.38

② 4.27 + 7.01

③ 4.7 + 3.3

④ 1.2 + 6.18

⑤ 1.1 + 4.72

⑥ 4.7 + 11.2

⑦ 0.7 + 4.63

⑧ 14.7 + 5.33

⑨ 2.2 + 13.84

⑩ 8.8 + 9

⑪ 9.3 + 4.01

⑫ 7 + 2.43

⑬ 15 – 2.2

⑭ 2.33 – 2.08

⑮ 13.5 – 1.33

⑯ 8.5 – 5.71

⑰ 5 – 4.32

⑱ 6.6 – 1.68

⑲ 5.63 – 1.89

⑳ 7.23 – 4

㉑ 21.8 – 4.70

㉒ 7.57 – 3.4

㉓ 5.6 – 4.1

㉔ 55.2 – 3.81

© Libro Studio LLC 2020

Name: _____

Score:

① $0.48 + 0.43$

② $3.12 + 1.2$

③ $1.13 + 4.71$

④ $6.14 + 3.12$

⑤ $7.89 + 1.6$

⑥ $16.3 + 5.8$

⑦ $2.6 + 2$

⑧ $3.2 + 40.05$

⑨ $2.4 + 0.68$

⑩ $3.1 + 1.38$

⑪ $7.97 + 6.4$

⑫ $60.5 + 5.3$

⑬ $7 - 0.59$

⑭ $9.5 - 2.13$

⑮ $6.3 - 1.88$

⑯ $64.2 - 59.8$

⑰ $5.8 - 0.98$

⑱ $5.72 - 2.7$

⑲ $36.05 - 2.28$

⑳ $8.2 - 0.55$

㉑ $9.12 - 5.6$

㉒ $10 - 9.87$

㉓ $6.49 - 0.62$

㉔ $7.1 - 4.18$

© Libro Studio LLC 2020

Name: _____

Score:

1/4 % 5.3 x 3.107 290 = 8

① 9.01 + 8.07　　② 7.3 + 3.12　　③ 3.7 + 12.8　　④ 0.29 + 4.18

⑤ 8.1 + 0.21　　⑥ 7.7 + 6.14　　⑦ 1.2 + 2.18　　⑧ 7.38 + 1.23

⑨ 3.89 + 6.08　　⑩ 8.2 + 1.19　　⑪ 9.82 + 3.64　　⑫ 2.23 + 2.6

⑬ 3.7 − 3.64　　⑭ 13.22 − 8.31　　⑮ 6.32 − 2.35　　⑯ 83.2 − 10.3

⑰ 7.27 − 3.2　　⑱ 5.9 − 3.24　　⑲ 3.5 − 2.21　　⑳ 10.6 − 1.4

㉑ 13.27 − 8.4　　㉒ 5.3 − 0.06　　㉓ 1.04 − 0.95　　㉔ 5.57 − 3.27

© Libro Studio LLC 2020

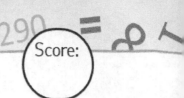

Name: _____

Score:

Multiplying Powers of 10

Steps:		1. Count the zeros in the power of 10.	2. Move the decimal that many spaces to the right. *(add zeros as place holders if needed.)*	3. Answer
Example 1:	10 x 8.5	10 (one zero)	8.5	85
Example 2:	6.42 x 1000	1000 (three zeros)	6.420	6,420

① **6.57 x 10**

② **1,000 x 1.5**

③ **100 x 52.6**

④ **10 x 8.2**

⑤ **0.132 x 10**

⑥ **0.38 x 1,000**

⑦ **100 x 42.4**

⑧ **97.57 x 10**

⑨ **100 x 9.708**

⑩ **1,000 x 6.1**

⑪ **10,000 x 7.4**

⑫ **28.01 x 10**

⑬ **1,000 x 0.32**

⑭ **44.05 x 100**

⑮ **10 x 0.05**

⑯ **100 x 72.4**

© Libro Studio LLC 2020

Day 32
Multiplying Decimals

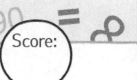

Name: _____

Score:

① 9.6 x 100

② 0.5 x 1,000

③ 0.25 x 10

④ 1,000 x 1.5

⑤ 10,000 x 6.28

⑥ 10 x 4.3

⑦ 10 x 0.05

⑧ 8.31 x 100

⑨ 9.3 x 1,000

⑩ 10 x 2.208

⑪ 2.27 x 1,000

⑫ 2.5 x 100

⑬ 100 x 11.6

⑭ 10 x 3.52

⑮ 13.7 x 1,000

⑯ 10 x 7.23

⑰ 8.3 x 10,000

⑱ 100 x 6.21

⑲ 1,000 x 0.2

⑳ 0.3 x 10

㉑ 0.76 x 10

㉒ 0.005 x 10

㉓ 9.71 x 100

㉔ 8.1 x 1,000

© Libro Studio LLC 2020

Name: _____

Score:

Steps:	1. Do not line up the decimals.	2. Solve like a normal problem.	3. Place the decimal by counting how many decimal places were in the problem.
Example: 0.79 x 6.5	0.79 x 6.5	0.79 x 6.5 395 + 4740 5135	(2 decimal places) 0.79 (1 decimal place) x 6.5 395 + 4740 (3 decimal places) 5.135

① 6.57 x 0.3

② 9.002 x 1.5

③ 0.49 x 52.6

④ 5.7 x 8.2

⑤ 132 x 6.6

⑥ 0.38 x 4.97

⑦ 2.6 x 42.4

⑧ 97.57 x 0.8

⑨ 3.41 x 9.708

⑩ 3.02 x 6.1

⑪ 5 x 7.4

⑫ 28.01 x 0.9

⑬ 1.61 x 0.32

⑭ 44.05 x 2.6

⑮ 7.8 x 0.05

⑯ 6.55 x 72.4

© Libro Studio LLC 2020

Day 34
Multiplying Decimals

Name: _____

Score:

① 150 x 0.5

② 50 x 1.5

③ 8 x 4.61

④ 4.3 x 2.81

⑤ 7.3 x 8.3

⑥ 9.16 x 10

⑦ 12 x 0.2

⑧ 0.02 x 100

⑨ 7.6 x 4.8

⑩ 3.82 x 7.62

⑪ 15 x 0.2

⑫ 20.4 x 5.7

⑬ 0.37 x 10

⑭ 5.4 x 8.72

⑮ 27 x 3.18

⑯ 9.01 x 7.5

⑰ 2.7 x 2.13

⑱ 8.7 x 100

⑲ 30 x 7.24

⑳ 2.2 x 3.5

㉑ 4.78 x 2.37

㉒ 2.7 x 1.209

㉓ 2 x 1.32

㉔ 6.1 x 8.25

© Libro Studio LLC 2020

Name: _____

Score:

① 9.6 x 2.56

② 0.5 x 40

③ 0.25 x 8

④ 2 x 1.5

⑤ 7.7 x 6.28

⑥ 8.6 x 4.3

⑦ 9.01 x 0.05

⑧ 8.31 x 3.62

⑨ 9.3 x 3.1

⑩ 3.3 x 100

⑪ 2.27 x 28

⑫ 2.5 x 5

⑬ 9.25 x 11.6

⑭ 6.1 x 3.52

⑮ 13.7 x 3.93

⑯ 4.4 x 7.23

⑰ 8.3 x 5.71

⑱ 9 x 6.21

⑲ 1,000 x 0.2

⑳ 0.3 x 100

㉑ 0.76 x 11.5

㉒ 60 x 2.1

㉓ 9.71 x 5.4

㉔ 8.1 x 3.3

© Libro Studio LLC 2020

Day 36
Multiplying Decimals

Name: _____

Score:

① 7.12 x 4.12

② 6.12 x 3.1

③ 8.32 x 2.77

④ 1.27 x 2.88

⑤ 4.7 x 2.12

⑥ 1.7 x 9.605

⑦ 3.6 x 5.34

⑧ 9.3 x 5.83

⑨ 9.23 x 6

⑩ 22.1 x 9.12

⑪ 3.12 x 7.18

⑫ 10 x 2.12

⑬ 1,000 x 4.55

⑭ 6.28 x 4.52

⑮ 64.2 x 1.77

⑯ 5.3 x 2.7

⑰ 9.21 x 2.92

⑱ 8.48 x 6.3

⑲ 9.2 x 3.9

⑳ 2.1 x 8.73

㉑ 10 x 1.22

㉒ 8.2 x 2.48

㉓ 5.162 x 3

㉔ 1.27 x 1.24

© Libro Studio LLC 2020

Day 37
Multiplying Decimals

Name: _____

Score:

① 36 x 2.12

② 8.2 x 6.23

③ 0.74 x 4.92

④ 2 x 3.23

⑤ 9.12 x 10

⑥ 8.31 x 74

⑦ 8.102 x 2.1

⑧ 6.23 x 2.56

⑨ 4.1 x 2.31

⑩ 1.82 x 6.34

⑪ 9.52 x 4.65

⑫ 6.54 x 17.5

⑬ 9.31 x 1.86

⑭ 1.23 x 5.48

⑮ 1.58 x 1.05

⑯ 10.3 x 3.1

⑰ 27.6 x 1.16

⑱ 1.74 x 2.9

⑲ 1.27 x 4.11

⑳ 10 x 8.76

㉑ 6.07 x 0.28

㉒ 2.47 x 100

㉓ 4.02 x 1.01

㉔ 7.3 x 11.2

© Libro Studio LLC 2020

Name: _____

Score: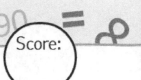

① 5.26 x 2.11

② 0.631 x 20

③ 5.8 x 2.71

④ 6.2 x 9.3

⑤ 6.31 x 0.06

⑥ 8.8 x 7.28

⑦ 1.98 x 0.3

⑧ 100 x 6.23

⑨ 89 x 2.91

⑩ 12.3 x 5.2

⑪ 74.21 x 1.6

⑫ 6.39 x 5.7

⑬ 50 x 0.7

⑭ 7.25 x 9.4

⑮ 3.61 x 10

⑯ 2.751 x 3

⑰ 11.5 x 6.6

⑱ 5.34 x 9.8

⑲ 20 x 0.8

⑳ 6.2 x 17.6

㉑ 1.52 x 10

㉒ 5.5 x 3.72

㉓ 0.4 x 0.05

㉔ 6.07 x 9

© Libro Studio LLC 2020

Name: _____

Score: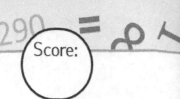

Problems 1-24: *Convert the percent to a decimal, then multiply.*

① 70% x 2.92

② 7.5 x 200%

③ 10% x 2.33

④ 50 x 2%

⑤ 50% x 60

⑥ 25% x 500

⑦ 130% x 67.8

⑧ 6% x 3200

⑨ 7 x 800%

⑩ 13% x 12.5

⑪ 100% x 4.44

⑫ 10 x 35%

⑬ 0.8% x 2

⑭ 100 x 93%

⑮ 5 x 400%

⑯ 1500 x 90%

⑰ 65 x 7.5%

⑱ 75% x 120

⑲ 5% x 20

⑳ 30 x 20%

㉑ 89% x 50.8

㉒ ⁴ 48 x 55%

㉓ 27% x 900

㉔ 5 x 300%

© Libro Studio LLC 2020

Day 40
Multiplying Decimals

© Libro Studio LLC 2020

Name: _____

Score:

Problems 1-24: *Convert the percent to a decimal, then multiply.*

① 100% x 4.8

② 40 x 50%

③ 150% x 6.55

④ 300 x 20%

⑤ 70% x 100

⑥ 75% x 400

⑦ 250% x 50

⑧ 11% x 600

⑨ 38 x 22%

⑩ 15% x 10

⑪ 160% x 2.91

⑫ 20 x 14%

⑬ 500% x 4

⑭ 0.5 x 93%

⑮ 1 x 900%

⑯ 350 x 120%

⑰ 32 x 76%

⑱ 8.4% x 50

⑲ 65% x 80

⑳ 30 x 60%

㉑ 44% x 10.2

㉒ 8 x 25%

㉓ 220% x 200

㉔ 12 x 300%

Day 41

Dividing Decimals

Name: _____

Score:

Dividing Powers of 10

Steps:		1. Count the zeros in the power of 10.	2. Move the decimal that many spaces to the left. *(add zeros as place holders if needed.)*	3. Answer
Example 1:	$10 \div 27.1$	10 (one zero)	27.1	2.71
Example 2:	$23.9 \div 1000$	1000 (three zeros)	23.9	0.0239

① $40.8 \div 100$

② $29.72 \div 10$

③ $20.60 \div 1,000$

④ $15.96 \div 10$

⑤ $1.4 \div 100$

⑥ $0.7 \div 100$

⑦ $31.05 \div 10$

⑧ $4.7 \div 1,000$

⑨ $1.76 \div 10$

⑩ $116.5 \div 10$

⑪ $2.2 \div 1,000$

⑫ $0.07 \div 1,000$

⑬ $209.6 \div 1,000$

⑭ $0.32 \div 100$

⑮ $185.5 \div 10$

⑯ $49.2 \div 100$

© Libro Studio LLC 2020

Name: _____

Score:

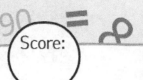

① 27.96 ÷ 10

② 161.16 ÷ 100

③ 45.64 ÷ 1,000

④ 104 ÷ 10

⑤ 204.48 ÷ 10

⑥ 136.92 ÷ 1,000

⑦ 58 ÷ 1,000

⑧ 46.5 ÷ 100

⑨ 813.2 ÷ 100

⑩ 327 ÷ 10

⑪ 325.71 ÷ 100

⑫ 509.6 ÷ 1,000

⑬ 5.02 ÷ 10

⑭ 58.52 ÷ 10

⑮ 1.7 ÷ 1,000

⑯ 78.8 ÷ 100

⑰ 185.8 ÷ 1,000

⑱ 121.9 ÷ 100

⑲ 69.41 ÷ 10

⑳ 1.70 ÷ 100

㉑ 410.4 ÷ 10

㉒ 17.74 ÷ 10

㉓ 4.26 ÷ 100

㉔ 20.9 ÷ 1,000

© Libro Studio LLC 2020

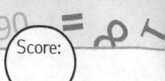

Name: _____

Score:

① 31.36 ÷ 100

② 129.32 ÷ 10

③ 413.5 ÷ 1,000

④ 20.56 ÷ 10

⑤ 153 ÷ 1,000

⑥ 274 ÷ 10

⑦ 6.36 ÷ 100

⑧ 18.62 ÷ 10

⑨ 12 ÷ 10

⑩ 5 ÷ 100

⑪ 90.20 ÷ 100

⑫ 116.6 ÷ 1,000

⑬ 55.80 ÷ 100

⑭ 2.87 ÷ 100

⑮ 124.74 ÷ 10

⑯ 65.52 ÷ 1,000

⑰ 43.68 ÷ 1,000

⑱ 9.31 ÷ 10

⑲ 44.46 ÷ 100

⑳ 94 ÷ 10

㉑ 526.5 ÷ 10

㉒ 140.7 ÷ 100

㉓ 89.91 ÷ 10

㉔ 77.81 ÷ 1,000

© Libro Studio LLC 2020

Name: _____

Score:

Steps:	1. Rewrite the problem. Move both decimals until the numerator is a whole number.	2. Solve like a normal division problem.	3. Place the decimal in the answer, straight above the decimal in the numerator.

Example: $34.65 \div 1.5$

$1.5\overline{)34.65}$

$$\begin{array}{r} 23\ 1 \\ 15\overline{)346.5} \\ -30 \\ \hline 46 \\ -45 \\ \hline 1\ 5 \\ -1\ 5 \\ \hline 0 \end{array}$$

$$\begin{array}{r} 23.1 \\ 15\overline{)346.5} \\ -30 \\ \hline 46 \\ -45 \\ \hline 1\ 5 \\ -1\ 5 \\ \hline 0 \end{array}$$

① $70.3 \div 3.7$

② $21.24 \div 0.36$

③ $66.15 \div 9.8$

④ $43.32 \div 0.57$

⑤ $32.76 \div 2.1$

⑥ $11.532 \div 1.24$

⑦ $2.996 \div 7$

⑧ $79.625 \div 24.5$

⑨ $239.86 \div 6.7$

⑩ $0.48 \div 0.6$

⑪ $6.93 \div 5.5$

⑫ $77.28 \div 0.84$

⑬ $6.05 \div 5$

⑭ $131.6 \div 4.7$

⑮ $38.08 \div 8$

⑯ $16.06 \div 2.2$

© Libro Studio LLC 2020

Name: _____

Score:

① 73.8 ÷ 12.3

② 24.22 ÷ 2

③ 405.6 ÷ 52

④ 2.32 ÷ 1.16

⑤ 75.90 ÷ 2.3

⑥ 2.28 ÷ 1.14

⑦ 13.68 ÷ 1.14

⑧ 56.64 ÷ 6

⑨ 7.98 ÷ 1.14

⑩ 84.5 ÷ 1.3

⑪ 16.96 ÷ 8

⑫ 41.4 ÷ 12

⑬ 65.68 ÷ 8

⑭ 356.5 ÷ 1.55

⑮ 6.82 ÷ 2

⑯ 69.3 ÷ 3

⑰ 7.77 ÷ 7

⑱ 42.98 ÷ 7

⑲ 46.35 ÷ 5

⑳ 43.26 ÷ 6

㉑ 83.16 ÷ 1.32

㉒ 73.8 ÷ 6

㉓ 28.8 ÷ 9

㉔ 18.26 ÷ 2

© Libro Studio LLC 2020

Day 46
Dividing Decimals

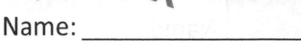
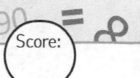

Name: _____

Score:

① 15.45 ÷ 5

② 22.24 ÷ 8

③ 11.64 ÷ 4

④ 20.51 ÷ 7

⑤ 5.48 ÷ 2

⑥ 66.01 ÷ 23

⑦ 11.16 ÷ 4

⑧ 8.8 ÷ 3.20

⑨ 3.75 ÷ 1.25

⑩ 14.55 ÷ 5

⑪ 21.28 ÷ 2.66

⑫ 45.18 ÷ 2.51

⑬ 107.8 ÷ 2.2

⑭ 8.2 ÷ 4.1

⑮ 12.22 ÷ 2

⑯ 51.98 ÷ 1.13

⑰ 55.8 ÷ 3.1

⑱ 25.3 ÷ 2.3

⑲ 113.68 ÷ 8.12

⑳ 46.8 ÷ 3.12

㉑ 23.1 ÷ 2.31

㉒ 21.98 ÷ 7

㉓ 197.34 ÷ 23

㉔ 19.28 ÷ 8

© Libro Studio LLC 2020

Name: _____

Score:

① 1.1 ÷ 1.1

② 10.08 ÷ 1.12

③ 16.8 ÷ 2.1

④ 7.84 ÷ 1.12

⑤ 46.16 ÷ 8

⑥ 12.22 ÷ 6.11

⑦ 24.88 ÷ 6.22

⑧ 22.20 ÷ 2.22

⑨ 48.60 ÷ 8.1

⑩ 3.69 ÷ 1.23

⑪ 16.98 ÷ 6

⑫ 13.56 ÷ 2

⑬ 8.79 ÷ 3

⑭ 8.16 ÷ 3

⑮ 53.92 ÷ 8

⑯ 5.98 ÷ 2

⑰ 2.02 ÷ 2

⑱ 49.6 ÷ 6.2

⑲ 5.7 ÷ 1.14

⑳ 75.96 ÷ 6.33

㉑ 84 ÷ 4.2

㉒ 20.16 ÷ 1.12

㉓ 0.68 ÷ 2

㉔ 7.68 ÷ 8

© Libro Studio LLC 2020

Day 48
Dividing Decimals

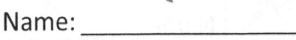

Name: _____

Score:

① 29.12 ÷ 1.12

② 43.2 ÷ 3.6

③ 36.96 ÷ 2.31

④ 56.97 ÷ 2.11

⑤ 7.71 ÷ 3

⑥ 62.16 ÷ 2.22

⑦ 23.31 ÷ 1.11

⑧ 28.99 ÷ 2.23

⑨ 34.32 ÷ 12

⑩ 13.90 ÷ 5

⑪ 19.11 ÷ 7

⑫ 14.55 ÷ 5

⑬ 22.88 ÷ 8

⑭ 25.11 ÷ 9

⑮ 47.64 ÷ 6

⑯ 8.67 ÷ 3

⑰ 15.35 ÷ 5

⑱ 11.68 ÷ 4

⑲ 26.64 ÷ 2.22

⑳ 133.25 ÷ 5.33

㉑ 170.66 ÷ 3.22

㉒ 1.15 ÷ 5

㉓ 10.5 ÷ 5

㉔ 16.96 ÷ 2.12

© Libro Studio LLC 2020

Day 49
Dividing Decimals

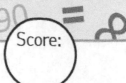

Name: _____

Score:

① 86.8 ÷ 6.2

② 18.9 ÷ 9

③ 3.2 ÷ 8

④ 31.36 ÷ 1.12

⑤ 69.30 ÷ 2.1

⑥ 11.10 ÷ 2.22

⑦ 150.96 ÷ 8.88

⑧ 6.36 ÷ 2.12

⑨ 85.2 ÷ 3.55

⑩ 435.4 ÷ 6.22

⑪ 97.44 ÷ 3.36

⑫ 168.91 ÷ 8.89

⑬ 379.8 ÷ 6.33

⑭ 296.02 ÷ 3.61

⑮ 20.88 ÷ 5.22

⑯ 52.46 ÷ 1.22

⑰ 135.42 ÷ 2.22

⑱ 15.12 ÷ 6

⑲ 6.21 ÷ 9

⑳ 19.32 ÷ 3.22

㉑ 1.40 ÷ 5

㉒ 19.32 ÷ 6.44

㉓ 75.71 ÷ 1.13

㉔ 40.60 ÷ 5

© Libro Studio LLC 2020

Day 50
Dividing Decimals

Name: _____

Score:

① 6 ÷ 1.14

② 132.93 ÷ 2.11

③ 25.63 ÷ 2.33

④ 6 ÷ 2.1

⑤ 23.88 ÷ 3

⑥ 73.5 ÷ 9.8

⑦ 15.68 ÷ 1.12

⑧ 12.3 ÷ 1.5

⑨ 6.99 ÷ 2.33

⑩ 94.43 ÷ 1.33

⑪ 6.99 ÷ 2.33

⑫ 95.76 ÷ 1.33

⑬ 333.94 ÷ 5.66

⑭ 82.88 ÷ 1.12

⑮ 173.88 ÷ 3.22

⑯ 41.44 ÷ 56

⑰ 230.88 ÷ 3.12

⑱ 107.52 ÷ 5.12

⑲ 113.22 ÷ 2.22

⑳ 487.60 ÷ 9.2

㉑ 176.25 ÷ 2.35

㉒ 193.44 ÷ 3.12

㉓ 9.31 ÷ 1.33

㉔ 158.44 ÷ 2.33

© Libro Studio LLC 2020

Name: _____

Score:

Steps:	1. Divide the top and bottom by the greatest common denominator.	2. If the top number is larger than the bottom, divide it by the bottom to make whole numbers.	3. Write the reduced fraction.
Example 1:	$\dfrac{8}{10}$ $\dfrac{8 \div 2 = 4}{10 \div 2 = 5}$		$\dfrac{8}{10} = \left(\dfrac{4}{5}\right)$
Example 2: Whole numbers	$\dfrac{30}{9}$ $\dfrac{30 \div 3 = 10}{9 \div 3 = 3}$	$10 \div 3 = 3 \text{ R } 1$	$\dfrac{30}{9} = \left(3\dfrac{1}{3}\right)$

Problems 1-16: *Reduce each fraction to its lowest term.*

① $\dfrac{2}{4}$

② $\dfrac{5}{20}$

③ $\dfrac{2}{8}$

④ $\dfrac{4}{36}$

⑤ $\dfrac{6}{4}$

⑥ $\dfrac{22}{5}$

⑦ $\dfrac{10}{8}$

⑧ $\dfrac{28}{4}$

⑨ $\dfrac{10}{100}$

⑩ $\dfrac{3}{18}$

⑪ $\dfrac{2}{48}$

⑫ $\dfrac{5}{80}$

⑬ $\dfrac{42}{5}$

⑭ $\dfrac{19}{6}$

⑮ $\dfrac{25}{9}$

⑯ $\dfrac{7}{6}$

© Libro Studio LLC 2020

Name: _____

Score:

Problems 1-24: *Reduce each fraction to its lowest term.*

① $\dfrac{15}{6}$ ② $\dfrac{3}{9}$ ③ $\dfrac{10}{25}$ ④ $\dfrac{4}{3}$

⑤ $\dfrac{24}{100}$ ⑥ $\dfrac{9}{2}$ ⑦ $\dfrac{4}{8}$ ⑧ $\dfrac{4}{12}$

⑨ $\dfrac{7}{49}$ ⑩ $\dfrac{27}{6}$ ⑪ $\dfrac{14}{3}$ ⑫ $\dfrac{5}{30}$

⑬ $\dfrac{6}{27}$ ⑭ $\dfrac{10}{42}$ ⑮ $\dfrac{9}{4}$ ⑯ $\dfrac{8}{26}$

⑰ $\dfrac{17}{5}$ ⑱ $\dfrac{8}{34}$ ⑲ $\dfrac{28}{100}$ ⑳ $\dfrac{55}{9}$

㉑ $\dfrac{24}{7}$ ㉒ $\dfrac{3}{15}$ ㉓ $\dfrac{10}{65}$ ㉔ $\dfrac{20}{50}$

© Libro Studio LLC 2020

Name: _____

Score:

Problems 1-24: *Reduce each fraction to its lowest term.*

① $\dfrac{27}{18}$　　② $\dfrac{12}{54}$　　③ $\dfrac{11}{6}$　　④ $\dfrac{5}{225}$

⑤ $\dfrac{12}{16}$　　⑥ $\dfrac{9}{21}$　　⑦ $\dfrac{6}{28}$　　⑧ $\dfrac{15}{27}$

⑨ $\dfrac{102}{4}$　　⑩ $\dfrac{100}{1000}$　　⑪ $\dfrac{38}{7}$　　⑫ $\dfrac{25}{90}$

⑬ $\dfrac{24}{54}$　　⑭ $\dfrac{9}{42}$　　⑮ $\dfrac{7}{5}$　　⑯ $\dfrac{18}{10}$

⑰ $\dfrac{2}{56}$　　⑱ $\dfrac{13}{5}$　　⑲ $\dfrac{16}{40}$　　⑳ $\dfrac{12}{60}$

㉑ $\dfrac{50}{40}$　　㉒ $\dfrac{25}{3}$　　㉓ $\dfrac{8}{22}$　　㉔ $\dfrac{19}{5}$

© Libro Studio LLC 2020

Day 54
Reducing Fractions

Name: _____

Score:

Problems 1-24: *Reduce each fraction to its lowest term.*

① $\dfrac{32}{36}$

② $\dfrac{5}{100}$

③ $\dfrac{12}{72}$

④ $\dfrac{28}{6}$

⑤ $\dfrac{3}{2}$

⑥ $\dfrac{10}{120}$

⑦ $\dfrac{54}{18}$

⑧ $\dfrac{82}{3}$

⑨ $\dfrac{15}{9}$

⑩ $\dfrac{32}{7}$

⑪ $\dfrac{13}{4}$

⑫ $\dfrac{16}{3}$

⑬ $\dfrac{20}{45}$

⑭ $\dfrac{58}{25}$

⑮ $\dfrac{24}{40}$

⑯ $\dfrac{18}{63}$

⑰ $\dfrac{19}{7}$

⑱ $\dfrac{2}{12}$

⑲ $\dfrac{25}{200}$

⑳ $\dfrac{10}{3}$

㉑ $\dfrac{63}{12}$

㉒ $\dfrac{14}{63}$

㉓ $\dfrac{5}{4}$

㉔ $\dfrac{8}{12}$

© Libro Studio LLC 2020

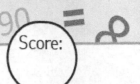

Name: _____

Score:

Problems 1-24: *Reduce each fraction to its lowest term.*

① $\dfrac{36}{72}$　　② $\dfrac{9}{4}$　　③ $\dfrac{2}{8}$　　④ $\dfrac{6}{60}$

⑤ $\dfrac{13}{7}$　　⑥ $\dfrac{20}{8}$　　⑦ $\dfrac{20}{100}$　　⑧ $\dfrac{16}{24}$

⑨ $\dfrac{8}{26}$　　⑩ $\dfrac{25}{30}$　　⑪ $\dfrac{7}{3}$　　⑫ $\dfrac{9}{33}$

⑬ $\dfrac{175}{25}$　　⑭ $\dfrac{42}{5}$　　⑮ $\dfrac{24}{28}$　　⑯ $\dfrac{17}{9}$

⑰ $\dfrac{56}{6}$　　⑱ $\dfrac{7}{35}$　　⑲ $\dfrac{2}{48}$　　⑳ $\dfrac{25}{10}$

㉑ $\dfrac{75}{15}$　　㉒ $\dfrac{11}{2}$　　㉓ $\dfrac{52}{20}$　　㉔ $\dfrac{15}{45}$

© Libro Studio LLC 2020

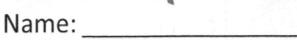
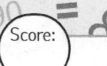

Name: _____

Score:

Problems 1-24: *Reduce each fraction to its lowest term.*

① $\dfrac{612}{50}$ ② $\dfrac{9}{2}$ ③ $\dfrac{8}{64}$ ④ $\dfrac{42}{49}$

⑤ $\dfrac{10}{130}$ ⑥ $\dfrac{72}{90}$ ⑦ $\dfrac{12}{21}$ ⑧ $\dfrac{4}{14}$

⑨ $\dfrac{6}{100}$ ⑩ $\dfrac{84}{25}$ ⑪ $\dfrac{9}{24}$ ⑫ $\dfrac{5}{70}$

⑬ $\dfrac{13}{4}$ ⑭ $\dfrac{3}{99}$ ⑮ $\dfrac{31}{6}$ ⑯ $\dfrac{25}{35}$

⑰ $\dfrac{53}{9}$ ⑱ $\dfrac{14}{42}$ ⑲ $\dfrac{68}{10}$ ⑳ $\dfrac{5}{2}$

㉑ $\dfrac{18}{7}$ ㉒ $\dfrac{24}{40}$ ㉓ $\dfrac{4}{22}$ ㉔ $\dfrac{25}{8}$

© Libro Studio LLC 2020

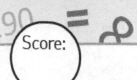

1/4 % 5.3 ✗ 3.107 290 = 8 ↑

Name: _____

Score:

Steps:	1. Multiply the top and bottom to find a common multiple	2. Solve like a normal addition or subtraction problem.	3. Reduce the fraction.
Example 1: **Addition**	$\frac{2}{3} + \frac{3}{4}$ $\quad$ $\frac{4 \times 2}{4 \times 3} + \frac{3 \times 3}{4 \times 3}$	$\frac{8}{12} + \frac{9}{12} = \frac{17}{12}$	$\frac{17}{12} = 1\frac{5}{12}$
Example 2: **Subtraction**	$\frac{7}{10} - \frac{1}{2}$ $\quad$ $\frac{7}{10} - \frac{1 \times 5}{2 \times 5}$	$\frac{7}{10} - \frac{5}{10} = \frac{2}{10}$	$\frac{2}{10} = \frac{1}{5}$

① $\frac{2}{6} + \frac{4}{5}$

② $\frac{1}{4} + \frac{5}{8}$

③ $\frac{1}{2} + \frac{2}{5}$

④ $\frac{7}{12} + \frac{3}{4}$

⑤ $\frac{5}{9} + \frac{5}{6}$

⑥ $\frac{1}{3} + \frac{3}{5}$

⑦ $\frac{4}{10} + \frac{1}{6}$

⑧ $\frac{1}{9} + \frac{2}{3}$

⑨ $\frac{9}{10} - \frac{1}{4}$

⑩ $\frac{1}{3} - \frac{2}{7}$

⑪ $\frac{5}{8} - \frac{1}{12}$

⑫ $\frac{3}{4} - \frac{3}{7}$

⑬ $\frac{2}{3} - \frac{1}{2}$

⑭ $\frac{6}{8} - \frac{4}{9}$

⑮ $\frac{3}{10} - \frac{1}{5}$

⑯ $\frac{7}{8} - \frac{3}{4}$

© Libro Studio LLC 2020

Name: _____

Score:

① $\dfrac{3}{7} + \dfrac{8}{9}$ ② $\dfrac{2}{9} + \dfrac{8}{2}$ ③ $\dfrac{3}{9} + \dfrac{2}{5}$ ④ $\dfrac{9}{2} + \dfrac{4}{5}$

⑤ $\dfrac{7}{7} + \dfrac{3}{7}$ ⑥ $\dfrac{7}{8} + \dfrac{3}{4}$ ⑦ $\dfrac{4}{2} + \dfrac{6}{8}$ ⑧ $\dfrac{2}{2} + \dfrac{6}{4}$

⑨ $\dfrac{8}{3} + \dfrac{2}{7}$ ⑩ $\dfrac{3}{7} + \dfrac{2}{4}$ ⑪ $\dfrac{3}{4} + \dfrac{3}{7}$ ⑫ $\dfrac{2}{9} + \dfrac{2}{4}$

⑬ $\dfrac{5}{6} - \dfrac{3}{4}$ ⑭ $\dfrac{8}{9} - \dfrac{2}{7}$ ⑮ $\dfrac{7}{5} - \dfrac{3}{6}$ ⑯ $\dfrac{4}{7} - \dfrac{3}{7}$

⑰ $\dfrac{6}{3} - \dfrac{2}{6}$ ⑱ $\dfrac{8}{4} - \dfrac{5}{4}$ ⑲ $\dfrac{7}{8} - \dfrac{4}{9}$ ⑳ $\dfrac{3}{2} - \dfrac{2}{3}$

㉑ $\dfrac{6}{7} - \dfrac{2}{4}$ ㉒ $\dfrac{4}{8} - \dfrac{3}{10}$ ㉓ $\dfrac{8}{12} - \dfrac{5}{12}$ ㉔ $\dfrac{4}{6} - \dfrac{3}{7}$

© Libro Studio LLC 2020

Name: _____

Score:

① $\dfrac{5}{6} + \dfrac{6}{4}$

② $\dfrac{3}{4} + \dfrac{12}{3}$

③ $\dfrac{8}{4} + \dfrac{3}{6}$

④ $\dfrac{6}{2} + \dfrac{3}{7}$

⑤ $\dfrac{5}{4} + \dfrac{4}{2}$

⑥ $\dfrac{7}{3} + \dfrac{5}{4}$

⑦ $\dfrac{6}{4} + \dfrac{3}{2}$

⑧ $\dfrac{5}{2} + \dfrac{3}{6}$

⑨ $\dfrac{8}{3} + \dfrac{6}{5}$

⑩ $\dfrac{8}{3} + \dfrac{3}{4}$

⑪ $\dfrac{8}{12} + \dfrac{5}{4}$

⑫ $\dfrac{8}{4} + \dfrac{2}{6}$

⑬ $\dfrac{3}{5} - \dfrac{2}{4}$

⑭ $\dfrac{7}{3} - \dfrac{5}{3}$

⑮ $\dfrac{9}{6} - \dfrac{7}{8}$

⑯ $\dfrac{7}{9} - \dfrac{6}{11}$

⑰ $\dfrac{7}{4} - \dfrac{6}{4}$

⑱ $\dfrac{5}{3} - \dfrac{3}{2}$

⑲ $\dfrac{12}{9} - \dfrac{7}{7}$

⑳ $\dfrac{8}{5} - \dfrac{4}{4}$

㉑ $\dfrac{7}{8} - \dfrac{3}{7}$

㉒ $\dfrac{6}{6} - \dfrac{1}{5}$

㉓ $\dfrac{9}{8} - \dfrac{2}{3}$

㉔ $\dfrac{5}{6} - \dfrac{3}{4}$

© Libro Studio LLC 2020

① $\dfrac{7}{4} + \dfrac{4}{4}$

② $\dfrac{9}{6} + \dfrac{7}{5}$

③ $\dfrac{8}{6} + \dfrac{5}{4}$

④ $\dfrac{12}{9} + \dfrac{4}{8}$

⑤ $\dfrac{8}{8} + \dfrac{6}{4}$

⑥ $\dfrac{2}{9} + \dfrac{6}{4}$

⑦ $\dfrac{3}{4} + \dfrac{3}{9}$

⑧ $\dfrac{8}{7} + \dfrac{2}{4}$

⑨ $\dfrac{6}{3} + \dfrac{3}{6}$

⑩ $\dfrac{5}{3} + \dfrac{3}{7}$

⑪ $\dfrac{8}{4} + \dfrac{7}{4}$

⑫ $\dfrac{9}{4} + \dfrac{3}{12}$

⑬ $\dfrac{4}{8} - \dfrac{3}{9}$

⑭ $\dfrac{8}{5} - \dfrac{6}{4}$

⑮ $\dfrac{8}{4} - \dfrac{5}{4}$

⑯ $\dfrac{9}{7} - \dfrac{6}{8}$

⑰ $\dfrac{7}{9} - \dfrac{2}{3}$

⑱ $\dfrac{5}{6} - \dfrac{2}{7}$

⑲ $\dfrac{2}{4} - \dfrac{3}{8}$

⑳ $\dfrac{12}{10} - \dfrac{1}{2}$

㉑ $\dfrac{8}{5} - \dfrac{3}{10}$

㉒ $\dfrac{12}{9} - \dfrac{3}{4}$

㉓ $\dfrac{2}{4} - \dfrac{3}{7}$

㉔ $3 - \dfrac{5}{2}$

© Libro Studio LLC 2020

Name: _____

Score:

① $\dfrac{7}{3} + \dfrac{4}{4}$

② $\dfrac{5}{6} + \dfrac{4}{6}$

③ $\dfrac{7}{5} + \dfrac{6}{3}$

④ $\dfrac{4}{3} + \dfrac{4}{7}$

⑤ $\dfrac{8}{5} + \dfrac{1}{9}$

⑥ $\dfrac{9}{4} + \dfrac{4}{5}$

⑦ $\dfrac{3}{6} + \dfrac{4}{9}$

⑧ $\dfrac{8}{5} + \dfrac{4}{6}$

⑨ $\dfrac{8}{5} + \dfrac{3}{5}$

⑩ $\dfrac{7}{4} + \dfrac{3}{6}$

⑪ $\dfrac{4}{8} + \dfrac{6}{4}$

⑫ $\dfrac{9}{5} + \dfrac{3}{2}$

⑬ $\dfrac{9}{7} - \dfrac{7}{12}$

⑭ $\dfrac{8}{4} - \dfrac{5}{4}$

⑮ $\dfrac{4}{5} - \dfrac{3}{4}$

⑯ $\dfrac{5}{9} - \dfrac{3}{7}$

⑰ $\dfrac{12}{8} - \dfrac{3}{3}$

⑱ $\dfrac{4}{9} - \dfrac{3}{8}$

⑲ $\dfrac{4}{4} - \dfrac{3}{4}$

⑳ $\dfrac{12}{5} - \dfrac{6}{4}$

㉑ $\dfrac{8}{7} - \dfrac{3}{6}$

㉒ $\dfrac{6}{5} - \dfrac{4}{4}$

㉓ $\dfrac{8}{5} - \dfrac{4}{4}$

㉔ $\dfrac{3}{7} - \dfrac{1}{9}$

© Libro Studio LLC 2020

Name: _____

Score:

① $\dfrac{8}{12} + \dfrac{4}{4}$

② $\dfrac{5}{4} + \dfrac{4}{4}$

③ $\dfrac{7}{5} + \dfrac{3}{9}$

④ $\dfrac{7}{4} + \dfrac{3}{5}$

⑤ $\dfrac{4}{4} + \dfrac{3}{6}$

⑥ $\dfrac{3}{4} + \dfrac{2}{8}$

⑦ $\dfrac{8}{4} + \dfrac{3}{5}$

⑧ $\dfrac{4}{4} + \dfrac{3}{2}$

⑨ $\dfrac{8}{4} + \dfrac{3}{12}$

⑩ $\dfrac{2}{3} + \dfrac{3}{6}$

⑪ $\dfrac{6}{4} + \dfrac{3}{7}$

⑫ $\dfrac{4}{3} + \dfrac{3}{3}$

⑬ $\dfrac{7}{6} - \dfrac{5}{7}$

⑭ $\dfrac{9}{5} - \dfrac{3}{2}$

⑮ $\dfrac{3}{12} - \dfrac{2}{10}$

⑯ $\dfrac{8}{2} - \dfrac{3}{2}$

⑰ $\dfrac{9}{6} - \dfrac{7}{5}$

⑱ $\dfrac{8}{6} - \dfrac{4}{4}$

⑲ $\dfrac{7}{9} - \dfrac{3}{7}$

⑳ $\dfrac{3}{6} - \dfrac{3}{7}$

㉑ $\dfrac{9}{8} - \dfrac{5}{6}$

㉒ $\dfrac{4}{7} - \dfrac{1}{6}$

㉓ $\dfrac{6}{8} - \dfrac{2}{4}$

㉔ $\dfrac{8}{7} - \dfrac{4}{5}$

© Libro Studio LLC 2020

Day 63

Adding and Subtracting

Name: _____

Score:

① $\dfrac{6}{8} + \dfrac{2}{9}$

② $\dfrac{8}{5} + \dfrac{3}{7}$

③ $\dfrac{4}{4} + \dfrac{6}{5}$

④ $\dfrac{7}{6} + \dfrac{3}{9}$

⑤ $\dfrac{4}{6} + \dfrac{3}{9}$

⑥ $\dfrac{8}{4} + \dfrac{4}{5}$

⑦ $\dfrac{8}{4} + \dfrac{2}{8}$

⑧ $\dfrac{5}{9} + \dfrac{12}{8}$

⑨ $\dfrac{4}{4} + \dfrac{3}{5}$

⑩ $\dfrac{8}{3} + \dfrac{3}{9}$

⑪ $\dfrac{7}{9} + \dfrac{3}{5}$

⑫ $\dfrac{8}{4} + \dfrac{3}{6}$

⑬ $\dfrac{9}{5} - \dfrac{1}{2}$

⑭ $\dfrac{7}{5} - \dfrac{4}{3}$

⑮ $\dfrac{5}{4} - \dfrac{1}{3}$

⑯ $\dfrac{7}{6} - \dfrac{5}{8}$

⑰ $\dfrac{9}{8} - \dfrac{1}{6}$

⑱ $\dfrac{10}{9} - \dfrac{5}{7}$

⑲ $\dfrac{8}{6} - \dfrac{5}{4}$

⑳ $\dfrac{9}{12} - \dfrac{3}{5}$

㉑ $\dfrac{6}{4} - \dfrac{5}{4}$

㉒ $\dfrac{9}{8} - \dfrac{1}{5}$

㉓ $\dfrac{8}{12} - \dfrac{5}{10}$

㉔ $\dfrac{6}{8} - \dfrac{1}{4}$

© Libro Studio LLC 2020

Day 64
Adding and Subtracting

① $\dfrac{6}{5} + \dfrac{8}{4}$

② $\dfrac{9}{4} + \dfrac{3}{6}$

③ $\dfrac{5}{8} + \dfrac{9}{4}$

④ $\dfrac{8}{7} + \dfrac{5}{4}$

⑤ $\dfrac{6}{4} + \dfrac{3}{7}$

⑥ $\dfrac{7}{2} + \dfrac{5}{4}$

⑦ $\dfrac{6}{4} + \dfrac{9}{8}$

⑧ $\dfrac{2}{6} + \dfrac{3}{7}$

⑨ $\dfrac{7}{3} + \dfrac{8}{9}$

⑩ $\dfrac{3}{6} + \dfrac{2}{6}$

⑪ $\dfrac{7}{5} + \dfrac{2}{4}$

⑫ $\dfrac{2}{12} + \dfrac{12}{6}$

⑬ $\dfrac{12}{12} - \dfrac{8}{9}$

⑭ $\dfrac{9}{5} - \dfrac{7}{4}$

⑮ $\dfrac{8}{6} - \dfrac{2}{3}$

⑯ $\dfrac{9}{11} - \dfrac{3}{6}$

⑰ $\dfrac{9}{6} - \dfrac{1}{3}$

⑱ $\dfrac{12}{9} - \dfrac{10}{8}$

⑲ $\dfrac{6}{8} - \dfrac{3}{4}$

⑳ $\dfrac{6}{5} - \dfrac{2}{4}$

㉑ $\dfrac{9}{8} - \dfrac{3}{4}$

㉒ $\dfrac{12}{8} - \dfrac{7}{6}$

㉓ $\dfrac{6}{5} - \dfrac{1}{2}$

㉔ $\dfrac{7}{6} - \dfrac{4}{4}$

© Libro Studio LLC 2020

Name: _____

Score:

① $\dfrac{7}{5} + \dfrac{5}{4}$

② $\dfrac{8}{5} + \dfrac{6}{4}$

③ $\dfrac{9}{7} + \dfrac{4}{6}$

④ $\dfrac{9}{12} + \dfrac{7}{9}$

⑤ $\dfrac{8}{7} + \dfrac{6}{5}$

⑥ $\dfrac{8}{4} + \dfrac{4}{4}$

⑦ $\dfrac{9}{7} + \dfrac{8}{6}$

⑧ $\dfrac{12}{8} + \dfrac{9}{4}$

⑨ $\dfrac{12}{12} + \dfrac{9}{8}$

⑩ $\dfrac{6}{8} + \dfrac{5}{7}$

⑪ $\dfrac{8}{12} + \dfrac{9}{6}$

⑫ $\dfrac{8}{7} + \dfrac{4}{4}$

⑬ $\dfrac{6}{3} - \dfrac{3}{2}$

⑭ $\dfrac{8}{7} - \dfrac{3}{4}$

⑮ $\dfrac{9}{8} - \dfrac{4}{7}$

⑯ $\dfrac{8}{12} - \dfrac{1}{4}$

⑰ $\dfrac{6}{5} - \dfrac{2}{9}$

⑱ $\dfrac{8}{6} - \dfrac{5}{5}$

⑲ $\dfrac{7}{6} - \dfrac{6}{10}$

⑳ $\dfrac{8}{5} - \dfrac{1}{3}$

㉑ $\dfrac{9}{7} - \dfrac{7}{6}$

㉒ $\dfrac{5}{4} - \dfrac{2}{7}$

㉓ $\dfrac{4}{4} - \dfrac{2}{3}$

㉔ $\dfrac{8}{7} - \dfrac{3}{5}$

© Libro Studio LLC 2020

Name: _____

Score:

① $\dfrac{9}{6} + \dfrac{7}{4}$

② $\dfrac{8}{12} + \dfrac{9}{4}$

③ $\dfrac{5}{9} + \dfrac{3}{6}$

④ $\dfrac{8}{4} + \dfrac{2}{6}$

⑤ $\dfrac{8}{8} + \dfrac{8}{8}$

⑥ $\dfrac{5}{4} + \dfrac{4}{5}$

⑦ $\dfrac{7}{6} + \dfrac{2}{4}$

⑧ $\dfrac{2}{8} + \dfrac{6}{9}$

⑨ $\dfrac{5}{8} + \dfrac{9}{4}$

⑩ $\dfrac{8}{4} + \dfrac{7}{6}$

⑪ $\dfrac{4}{4} + \dfrac{3}{3}$

⑫ $\dfrac{8}{6} + \dfrac{3}{7}$

⑬ $\dfrac{8}{7} - \dfrac{1}{2}$

⑭ $\dfrac{5}{4} - \dfrac{5}{5}$

⑮ $\dfrac{9}{8} - \dfrac{3}{7}$

⑯ $\dfrac{6}{12} - \dfrac{1}{5}$

⑰ $\dfrac{8}{8} - \dfrac{3}{4}$

⑱ $\dfrac{2}{2} - \dfrac{1}{2}$

⑲ $\dfrac{6}{5} - \dfrac{2}{3}$

⑳ $\dfrac{9}{7} - \dfrac{6}{5}$

㉑ $\dfrac{6}{5} - \dfrac{4}{4}$

㉒ $\dfrac{6}{8} - \dfrac{3}{6}$

㉓ $\dfrac{6}{4} - \dfrac{5}{4}$

㉔ $\dfrac{8}{9} - \dfrac{5}{8}$

© Libro Studio LLC 2020

Name: _____

Score:

① $\dfrac{8}{4} + \dfrac{6}{12}$

② $\dfrac{6}{9} + \dfrac{8}{7}$

③ $\dfrac{9}{6} + \dfrac{5}{4}$

④ $\dfrac{3}{8} + \dfrac{3}{8}$

⑤ $\dfrac{4}{8} + \dfrac{6}{4}$

⑥ $\dfrac{12}{6} + \dfrac{3}{12}$

⑦ $\dfrac{9}{5} + \dfrac{3}{8}$

⑧ $\dfrac{2}{6} + \dfrac{4}{9}$

⑨ $\dfrac{8}{9} + \dfrac{5}{6}$

⑩ $\dfrac{3}{5} + \dfrac{7}{8}$

⑪ $\dfrac{9}{8} + \dfrac{5}{7}$

⑫ $\dfrac{8}{5} + \dfrac{6}{2}$

⑬ $\dfrac{8}{5} - \dfrac{4}{3}$

⑭ $\dfrac{9}{5} - \dfrac{6}{5}$

⑮ $\dfrac{8}{6} - \dfrac{5}{4}$

⑯ $\dfrac{8}{5} - \dfrac{6}{4}$

⑰ $\dfrac{8}{7} - \dfrac{3}{7}$

⑱ $\dfrac{5}{3} - \dfrac{3}{2}$

⑲ $\dfrac{9}{7} - \dfrac{6}{6}$

⑳ $\dfrac{8}{7} - \dfrac{1}{4}$

㉑ $\dfrac{6}{8} - \dfrac{4}{6}$

㉒ $\dfrac{9}{7} - \dfrac{5}{4}$

㉓ $\dfrac{8}{3} - \dfrac{7}{4}$

㉔ $\dfrac{6}{8} - \dfrac{3}{5}$

© Libro Studio LLC 2020

① $\dfrac{5}{12} + \dfrac{7}{8}$

② $\dfrac{8}{9} + \dfrac{4}{9}$

③ $\dfrac{2}{9} + \dfrac{8}{6}$

④ $\dfrac{7}{6} + \dfrac{9}{5}$

⑤ $\dfrac{8}{9} + \dfrac{3}{9}$

⑥ $\dfrac{6}{9} + \dfrac{3}{4}$

⑦ $\dfrac{8}{7} + \dfrac{5}{6}$

⑧ $\dfrac{9}{8} + \dfrac{5}{7}$

⑨ $\dfrac{9}{12} + \dfrac{5}{46}$

⑩ $\dfrac{9}{5} + \dfrac{3}{6}$

⑪ $\dfrac{12}{4} + \dfrac{7}{8}$

⑫ $\dfrac{8}{7} + \dfrac{6}{9}$

⑬ $\dfrac{8}{7} - \dfrac{4}{5}$

⑭ $\dfrac{6}{5} - \dfrac{4}{4}$

⑮ $\dfrac{9}{8} - \dfrac{5}{6}$

⑯ $\dfrac{1}{1} - \dfrac{1}{2}$

⑰ $\dfrac{10}{4} - \dfrac{3}{2}$

⑱ $\dfrac{9}{6} - \dfrac{5}{4}$

⑲ $\dfrac{7}{5} - \dfrac{4}{4}$

⑳ $\dfrac{8}{7} - \dfrac{1}{4}$

㉑ $\dfrac{9}{12} - \dfrac{5}{9}$

㉒ $\dfrac{6}{8} - \dfrac{3}{7}$

㉓ $\dfrac{8}{9} - \dfrac{5}{6}$

㉔ $\dfrac{8}{7} - \dfrac{5}{8}$

© Libro Studio LLC 2020

Name: _____

Score:

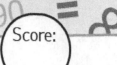

① $\dfrac{9}{6} + \dfrac{3}{6}$

② $\dfrac{9}{4} + \dfrac{3}{8}$

③ $\dfrac{7}{5} + \dfrac{6}{4}$

④ $\dfrac{7}{4} + \dfrac{9}{8}$

⑤ $\dfrac{4}{4} + \dfrac{7}{4}$

⑥ $\dfrac{8}{9} + \dfrac{6}{9}$

⑦ $\dfrac{8}{9} + \dfrac{5}{2}$

⑧ $\dfrac{7}{4} + \dfrac{4}{6}$

⑨ $\dfrac{7}{4} + \dfrac{4}{12}$

⑩ $\dfrac{5}{6} + \dfrac{3}{7}$

⑪ $\dfrac{6}{4} + \dfrac{9}{5}$

⑫ $\dfrac{4}{9} + \dfrac{2}{8}$

⑬ $\dfrac{6}{5} - \dfrac{4}{4}$

⑭ $\dfrac{7}{4} - \dfrac{6}{2}$

⑮ $\dfrac{9}{8} - \dfrac{2}{7}$

⑯ $\dfrac{5}{12} - \dfrac{2}{9}$

⑰ $\dfrac{8}{12} - \dfrac{3}{5}$

⑱ $\dfrac{8}{7} - \dfrac{1}{5}$

⑲ $\dfrac{8}{9} - \dfrac{3}{7}$

⑳ $\dfrac{6}{8} - \dfrac{6}{10}$

㉑ $\dfrac{9}{5} - \dfrac{6}{4}$

㉒ $\dfrac{8}{12} - \dfrac{3}{9}$

㉓ $\dfrac{8}{9} - \dfrac{3}{5}$

㉔ $\dfrac{8}{6} - \dfrac{7}{7}$

© Libro Studio LLC 2020

Name: _____

Score:

① $\dfrac{9}{12} + \dfrac{6}{4}$

② $\dfrac{8}{7} + \dfrac{3}{12}$

③ $\dfrac{6}{5} + \dfrac{3}{12}$

④ $\dfrac{7}{9} + \dfrac{3}{6}$

⑤ $\dfrac{9}{8} + \dfrac{5}{3}$

⑥ $\dfrac{5}{4} + \dfrac{3}{7}$

⑦ $\dfrac{8}{6} + \dfrac{4}{7}$

⑧ $\dfrac{8}{7} + \dfrac{8}{9}$

⑨ $\dfrac{6}{5} + \dfrac{8}{6}$

⑩ $\dfrac{7}{8} + \dfrac{6}{3}$

⑪ $\dfrac{12}{6} + \dfrac{7}{9}$

⑫ $\dfrac{3}{7} + \dfrac{8}{9}$

⑬ $\dfrac{12}{8} - \dfrac{6}{5}$

⑭ $\dfrac{7}{6} - \dfrac{1}{4}$

⑮ $\dfrac{8}{6} - \dfrac{6}{5}$

⑯ $\dfrac{9}{10} - \dfrac{7}{8}$

⑰ $\dfrac{6}{4} - \dfrac{5}{4}$

⑱ $\dfrac{9}{8} - \dfrac{3}{7}$

⑲ $\dfrac{10}{7} - \dfrac{5}{5}$

⑳ $\dfrac{9}{8} - \dfrac{4}{5}$

㉑ $\dfrac{6}{5} - \dfrac{4}{4}$

㉒ $\dfrac{8}{6} - \dfrac{5}{4}$

㉓ $\dfrac{3}{5} - \dfrac{1}{4}$

㉔ $\dfrac{9}{3} - \dfrac{2}{4}$

© Libro Studio LLC 2020

Name: _____

Score:

Steps:	(turn any whole number into a fraction)	1. Multiply the top numbers, then multiply the bottom numbers.	2. Reduce the fraction.
Example 1:	$\frac{2}{3} \times \frac{3}{4}$	$\frac{2 \times 3}{3 \times 4} = \frac{6}{12}$	$\frac{6}{12} = \frac{1}{2}$
Example 2: Whole number	$5 \times \frac{1}{2}$ $\quad \frac{5}{1} = \frac{1}{2}$	$\frac{5 \times 1}{1 \times 2} = \frac{5}{2}$	$2\frac{1}{2}$ *(already reduced)*

① $\frac{6}{7} \times \frac{3}{5}$

② $\frac{5}{8} \times \frac{1}{2}$

③ $\frac{4}{5} \times \frac{3}{5}$

④ $\frac{7}{9} \times \frac{2}{3}$

⑤ $3 \times \frac{3}{4}$

⑥ $\frac{3}{8} \times \frac{6}{7}$

⑦ $\frac{3}{6} \times 4$

⑧ $\frac{1}{4} \times \frac{7}{8}$

⑨ $\frac{1}{3} \times \frac{1}{3}$

⑩ $8 \times \frac{1}{6}$

⑪ $\frac{3}{8} \times \frac{1}{2}$

⑫ $\frac{5}{6} \times \frac{1}{3}$

⑬ $\frac{1}{4} \times \frac{3}{4}$

⑭ $\frac{6}{7} \times \frac{2}{5}$

⑮ $2 \times \frac{1}{4}$

⑯ $\frac{2}{3} \times \frac{3}{8}$

© Libro Studio LLC 2020

Day 72
Multiplying Fractions

① $\dfrac{5}{6} \times \dfrac{3}{9}$

② $\dfrac{7}{9} \times \dfrac{5}{3}$

③ $\dfrac{5}{3} \times \dfrac{7}{9}$

④ $3 \times \dfrac{6}{3}$

⑤ $\dfrac{9}{7} \times \dfrac{8}{3}$

⑥ $6 \times \dfrac{6}{3}$

⑦ $\dfrac{4}{6} \times \dfrac{2}{8}$

⑧ $\dfrac{5}{7} \times \dfrac{6}{4}$

⑨ $\dfrac{9}{9} \times \dfrac{10}{7}$

⑩ $6 \times \dfrac{8}{2}$

⑪ $\dfrac{4}{9} \times \dfrac{6}{7}$

⑫ $\dfrac{3}{2} \times \dfrac{8}{6}$

⑬ $\dfrac{4}{3} \times \dfrac{2}{6}$

⑭ $\dfrac{8}{7} \times \dfrac{6}{2}$

⑮ $\dfrac{6}{2} \times \dfrac{5}{9}$

⑯ $\dfrac{5}{8} \times \dfrac{9}{4}$

⑰ $5 \times \dfrac{7}{6}$

⑱ $\dfrac{7}{7} \times \dfrac{6}{5}$

⑲ $\dfrac{4}{3} \times \dfrac{9}{2}$

⑳ $9 \times \dfrac{9}{6}$

㉑ $\dfrac{3}{8} \times \dfrac{9}{2}$

㉒ $\dfrac{7}{6} \times \dfrac{5}{6}$

㉓ $4 \times \dfrac{7}{5}$

㉔ $\dfrac{4}{8} \times \dfrac{9}{5}$

© Libro Studio LLC 2020

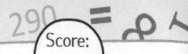

Day 73
Multiplying Fractions

Name: _____

Score:

① $\frac{7}{8} \times \frac{4}{5}$

② $\frac{8}{2} \times \frac{3}{5}$

③ $\frac{2}{3} \times \frac{2}{4}$

④ $\frac{8}{4} \times \frac{5}{6}$

⑤ $7 \times \frac{6}{4}$

⑥ $\frac{2}{7} \times \frac{3}{6}$

⑦ $\frac{7}{8} \times \frac{3}{7}$

⑧ $\frac{2}{4} \times \frac{9}{10}$

⑨ $\frac{3}{8} \times \frac{3}{5}$

⑩ $5 \times \frac{3}{2}$

⑪ $\frac{5}{2} \times \frac{2}{6}$

⑫ $\frac{2}{2} \times \frac{2}{2}$

⑬ $\frac{3}{3} \times \frac{3}{3}$

⑭ $\frac{4}{4} \times \frac{4}{4}$

⑮ $\frac{5}{5} \times \frac{5}{5}$

⑯ $\frac{8}{7} \times \frac{9}{6}$

⑰ $\frac{5}{4} \times \frac{3}{2}$

⑱ $\frac{2}{3} \times \frac{6}{8}$

⑲ $2 \times \frac{6}{9}$

⑳ $\frac{5}{6} \times \frac{8}{7}$

㉑ $\frac{8}{9} \times \frac{7}{5}$

㉒ $\frac{8}{7} \times \frac{6}{3}$

㉓ $\frac{2}{2} \times \frac{5}{5}$

㉔ $\frac{10}{9} \times \frac{3}{8}$

© Libro Studio LLC 2020

Day 74
Multiplying Fractions

Name: _____

Score:

① $\dfrac{8}{5} \times \dfrac{6}{7}$

② $\dfrac{2}{6} \times \dfrac{8}{2}$

③ $\dfrac{9}{3} \times \dfrac{3}{8}$

④ $\dfrac{5}{9} \times \dfrac{3}{9}$

⑤ $9 \times \dfrac{2}{7}$

⑥ $\dfrac{4}{6} \times \dfrac{3}{8}$

⑦ $\dfrac{9}{6} \times \dfrac{9}{7}$

⑧ $\dfrac{6}{8} \times \dfrac{4}{5}$

⑨ $\dfrac{9}{7} \times \dfrac{6}{4}$

⑩ $\dfrac{2}{3} \times \dfrac{3}{3}$

⑪ $\dfrac{2}{2} \times \dfrac{3}{2}$

⑫ $4 \times \dfrac{8}{5}$

⑬ $\dfrac{9}{7} \times \dfrac{3}{8}$

⑭ $\dfrac{5}{8} \times \dfrac{7}{9}$

⑮ $\dfrac{8}{4} \times \dfrac{3}{8}$

⑯ $\dfrac{9}{4} \times \dfrac{8}{6}$

⑰ $\dfrac{2}{5} \times \dfrac{2}{5}$

⑱ $\dfrac{4}{6} \times \dfrac{4}{6}$

⑲ $6 \times \dfrac{7}{9}$

⑳ $\dfrac{6}{8} \times \dfrac{8}{6}$

㉑ $7 \times \dfrac{5}{5}$

㉒ $\dfrac{6}{6} \times \dfrac{5}{10}$

㉓ $\dfrac{9}{4} \times \dfrac{8}{8}$

㉔ $\dfrac{2}{10} \times \dfrac{3}{3}$

© Libro Studio LLC 2020

Name: _____

Score:

① $\dfrac{6}{4} \times \dfrac{7}{2}$

② $2 \times \dfrac{4}{2}$

③ $\dfrac{2}{5} \times \dfrac{8}{10}$

④ $\dfrac{6}{9} \times \dfrac{3}{7}$

⑤ $\dfrac{9}{6} \times \dfrac{4}{9}$

⑥ $\dfrac{6}{5} \times \dfrac{3}{6}$

⑦ $6 \times \dfrac{9}{9}$

⑧ $\dfrac{9}{3} \times \dfrac{4}{2}$

⑨ $\dfrac{5}{9} \times \dfrac{3}{5}$

⑩ $3 \times \dfrac{8}{7}$

⑪ $3 \times \dfrac{3}{9}$

⑫ $3 \times \dfrac{8}{10}$

⑬ $\dfrac{8}{7} \times \dfrac{9}{9}$

⑭ $\dfrac{6}{2} \times \dfrac{7}{5}$

⑮ $\dfrac{3}{4} \times \dfrac{3}{6}$

⑯ $\dfrac{7}{4} \times \dfrac{9}{4}$

⑰ $\dfrac{8}{4} \times \dfrac{3}{8}$

⑱ $\dfrac{10}{5} \times \dfrac{6}{8}$

⑲ $9 \times \dfrac{2}{6}$

⑳ $\dfrac{8}{5} \times \dfrac{3}{4}$

㉑ $\dfrac{8}{4} \times \dfrac{3}{4}$

㉒ $\dfrac{5}{6} \times \dfrac{2}{5}$

㉓ $\dfrac{8}{10} \times \dfrac{9}{8}$

㉔ $\dfrac{8}{9} \times \dfrac{9}{4}$

© Libro Studio LLC 2020

Name: _____

Score:

① $\frac{6}{8} \times \frac{3}{5}$

② $\frac{9}{4} \times \frac{3}{5}$

③ $\frac{3}{4} \times \frac{3}{8}$

④ $\frac{6}{2} \times \frac{3}{4}$

⑤ $\frac{9}{8} \times \frac{3}{9}$

⑥ $7 \times \frac{3}{6}$

⑦ $\frac{9}{8} \times \frac{3}{9}$

⑧ $\frac{8}{5} \times \frac{3}{7}$

⑨ $\frac{5}{6} \times \frac{6}{5}$

⑩ $5 \times \frac{2}{5}$

⑪ $\frac{5}{6} \times \frac{8}{7}$

⑫ $\frac{9}{5} \times \frac{6}{3}$

⑬ $\frac{3}{6} \times \frac{8}{7}$

⑭ $\frac{5}{9} \times \frac{8}{4}$

⑮ $8 \times \frac{6}{4}$

⑯ $\frac{6}{5} \times \frac{2}{9}$

⑰ $\frac{9}{5} \times \frac{4}{7}$

⑱ $\frac{5}{4} \times \frac{2}{6}$

⑲ $\frac{6}{9} \times \frac{5}{3}$

⑳ $\frac{7}{6} \times \frac{3}{8}$

㉑ $\frac{9}{5} \times \frac{4}{9}$

㉒ $\frac{7}{2} \times \frac{6}{4}$

㉓ $\frac{5}{8} \times \frac{6}{9}$

㉔ $\frac{7}{5} \times \frac{5}{5}$

© Libro Studio LLC 2020

Name: _____

Score:

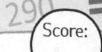

① $\dfrac{8}{4} \times \dfrac{6}{8}$

② $\dfrac{5}{6} \times \dfrac{3}{7}$

③ $3 \times \dfrac{6}{5}$

④ $\dfrac{5}{8} \times \dfrac{6}{2}$

⑤ $\dfrac{2}{7} \times \dfrac{5}{4}$

⑥ $\dfrac{4}{9} \times \dfrac{8}{7}$

⑦ $3 \times \dfrac{6}{8}$

⑧ $9 \times \dfrac{7}{5}$

⑨ $5 \times \dfrac{3}{9}$

⑩ $2 \times \dfrac{8}{2}$

⑪ $\dfrac{6}{9} \times \dfrac{5}{3}$

⑫ $9 \times \dfrac{4}{2}$

⑬ $\dfrac{9}{5} \times \dfrac{4}{6}$

⑭ $\dfrac{7}{5} \times \dfrac{6}{3}$

⑮ $\dfrac{2}{8} \times \dfrac{5}{9}$

⑯ $\dfrac{9}{6} \times \dfrac{3}{8}$

⑰ $\dfrac{3}{6} \times \dfrac{3}{5}$

⑱ $\dfrac{9}{7} \times \dfrac{5}{4}$

⑲ $\dfrac{2}{4} \times \dfrac{8}{10}$

⑳ $\dfrac{7}{4} \times \dfrac{5}{7}$

㉑ $5 \times \dfrac{3}{9}$

㉒ $\dfrac{6}{8} \times \dfrac{6}{9}$

㉓ $\dfrac{9}{6} \times \dfrac{5}{4}$

㉔ $\dfrac{5}{7} \times \dfrac{6}{2}$

© Libro Studio LLC 2020

Name: _____

Score:

① $3 \times \dfrac{3}{6}$

② $\dfrac{9}{5} \times \dfrac{8}{10}$

③ $10 \times \dfrac{6}{7}$

④ $\dfrac{3}{8} \times \dfrac{8}{7}$

⑤ $\dfrac{9}{4} \times \dfrac{6}{8}$

⑥ $\dfrac{10}{4} \times \dfrac{2}{4}$

⑦ $\dfrac{9}{8} \times \dfrac{3}{10}$

⑧ $\dfrac{7}{9} \times \dfrac{4}{8}$

⑨ $\dfrac{6}{4} \times \dfrac{4}{7}$

⑩ $\dfrac{7}{6} \times \dfrac{2}{7}$

⑪ $\dfrac{5}{2} \times \dfrac{2}{3}$

⑫ $\dfrac{8}{5} \times \dfrac{3}{9}$

⑬ $\dfrac{8}{9} \times \dfrac{3}{7}$

⑭ $8 \times \dfrac{2}{5}$

⑮ $\dfrac{2}{8} \times \dfrac{9}{6}$

⑯ $\dfrac{8}{6} \times \dfrac{5}{3}$

⑰ $7 \times \dfrac{5}{8}$

⑱ $\dfrac{5}{8} \times \dfrac{6}{7}$

⑲ $\dfrac{3}{8} \times \dfrac{9}{5}$

⑳ $\dfrac{3}{2} \times \dfrac{8}{9}$

㉑ $\dfrac{5}{4} \times \dfrac{8}{9}$

㉒ $\dfrac{7}{8} \times \dfrac{2}{7}$

㉓ $\dfrac{6}{9} \times \dfrac{7}{6}$

㉔ $8 \times \dfrac{5}{2}$

© Libro Studio LLC 2020

Day 79
Multiplying Fractions

① $\dfrac{4}{9} \times \dfrac{5}{5}$

② $\dfrac{6}{2} \times \dfrac{5}{8}$

③ $\dfrac{9}{4} \times \dfrac{8}{6}$

④ $\dfrac{8}{2} \times \dfrac{2}{5}$

⑤ $\dfrac{9}{7} \times \dfrac{6}{4}$

⑥ $\dfrac{3}{8} \times \dfrac{3}{8}$

⑦ $\dfrac{2}{8} \times \dfrac{7}{4}$

⑧ $2 \times \dfrac{3}{10}$

⑨ $4 \times \dfrac{3}{8}$

⑩ $\dfrac{9}{5} \times \dfrac{3}{6}$

⑪ $5 \times \dfrac{6}{2}$

⑫ $\dfrac{5}{9} \times \dfrac{6}{8}$

⑬ $\dfrac{8}{2} \times \dfrac{4}{9}$

⑭ $4 \times \dfrac{8}{9}$

⑮ $\dfrac{10}{2} \times \dfrac{5}{9}$

⑯ $\dfrac{9}{8} \times \dfrac{6}{5}$

⑰ $\dfrac{3}{5} \times \dfrac{6}{8}$

⑱ $\dfrac{8}{3} \times \dfrac{9}{7}$

⑲ $9 \times \dfrac{5}{3}$

⑳ $\dfrac{6}{4} \times \dfrac{8}{7}$

㉑ $\dfrac{5}{4} \times \dfrac{8}{7}$

㉒ $6 \times \dfrac{2}{8}$

㉓ $\dfrac{8}{10} \times \dfrac{5}{9}$

㉔ $\dfrac{5}{7} \times \dfrac{6}{8}$

© Libro Studio LLC 2020

Day 80
Multiplying Fractions

 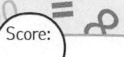

Name: _____

Score:

① $\dfrac{2}{4} \times \dfrac{8}{4}$

② $\dfrac{6}{9} \times \dfrac{3}{8}$

③ $\dfrac{7}{4} \times \dfrac{3}{6}$

④ $\dfrac{8}{3} \times \dfrac{9}{4}$

⑤ $8 \times \dfrac{3}{6}$

⑥ $\dfrac{4}{4} \times \dfrac{3}{9}$

⑦ $\dfrac{8}{4} \times \dfrac{3}{9}$

⑧ $\dfrac{4}{6} \times \dfrac{2}{3}$

⑨ $\dfrac{5}{4} \times \dfrac{7}{8}$

⑩ $2 \times \dfrac{3}{6}$

⑪ $4 \times \dfrac{3}{5}$

⑫ $\dfrac{4}{2} \times \dfrac{8}{3}$

⑬ $\dfrac{8}{2} \times \dfrac{3}{7}$

⑭ $\dfrac{4}{4} \times \dfrac{9}{8}$

⑮ $\dfrac{4}{2} \times \dfrac{9}{10}$

⑯ $\dfrac{9}{8} \times \dfrac{5}{7}$

⑰ $\dfrac{2}{6} \times \dfrac{5}{8}$

⑱ $\dfrac{7}{8} \times \dfrac{9}{4}$

⑲ $\dfrac{4}{2} \times \dfrac{5}{3}$

⑳ $\dfrac{4}{3} \times \dfrac{4}{3}$

㉑ $\dfrac{9}{6} \times \dfrac{5}{7}$

㉒ $\dfrac{6}{6} \times \dfrac{7}{8}$

㉓ $\dfrac{4}{2} \times \dfrac{4}{5}$

㉔ $\dfrac{9}{4} \times \dfrac{8}{5}$

© Libro Studio LLC 2020

$\frac{1}{4}$ $\%$ 5.3 $\times$ 3.107 290 = 8

Name: _____

Score:

Steps:	1. Flip the number you are dividing to make it a multiplication problem	2. Multiply the top numbers, then multiply the bottom numbers.	3. Reduce the fraction.
Example 1: Addition	$\frac{2}{3} \div \frac{2}{5}$ $\quad$ $\frac{2}{3} \times \frac{5}{2}$	$\frac{2 \times 5}{3 \times 2} = \frac{10}{6}$	$\frac{10}{6} = \frac{5}{3} = 1\frac{2}{3}$
Example 2: Subtraction	$\frac{7}{10} \div \frac{1}{2}$ $\quad$ $\frac{7}{10} \times \frac{2}{1}$	$\frac{7 \times 2}{10 \times 1} = \frac{14}{10}$	$\frac{14}{10} = \frac{7}{5} = 1\frac{2}{5}$

① $\frac{3}{4} \div \frac{1}{4}$

② $\frac{5}{6} \div \frac{1}{2}$

③ $\frac{7}{10} \div \frac{2}{5}$

④ $\frac{3}{4} \div \frac{3}{8}$

⑤ $\frac{5}{8} \div \frac{2}{5}$

⑥ $\frac{1}{2} \div \frac{1}{4}$

⑦ $6 \div \frac{1}{3}$

⑧ $\frac{3}{4} \div \frac{1}{2}$

⑨ $8 \div \frac{3}{4}$

⑩ $\frac{2}{4} \div \frac{3}{4}$

⑪ $\frac{2}{3} \div \frac{1}{7}$

⑫ $\frac{1}{4} \div 2$

⑬ $\frac{9}{10} \div \frac{5}{6}$

⑭ $\frac{1}{5} \div \frac{2}{9}$

⑮ $5 \div \frac{1}{2}$

⑯ $\frac{2}{3} \div \frac{7}{8}$

© Libro Studio LLC 2020

Name: _____

Score:

① $4 \div \dfrac{2}{5}$

② $\dfrac{6}{4} \div 2$

③ $\dfrac{2}{8} \div \dfrac{3}{7}$

④ $\dfrac{9}{2} \div \dfrac{3}{6}$

⑤ $5 \div \dfrac{2}{9}$

⑥ $\dfrac{4}{7} \div \dfrac{5}{4}$

⑦ $\dfrac{6}{5} \div \dfrac{3}{2}$

⑧ $\dfrac{4}{7} \div \dfrac{8}{4}$

⑨ $\dfrac{6}{4} \div \dfrac{3}{5}$

⑩ $\dfrac{8}{6} \div \dfrac{7}{4}$

⑪ $\dfrac{3}{9} \div \dfrac{8}{4}$

⑫ $\dfrac{5}{9} \div \dfrac{7}{4}$

⑬ $\dfrac{8}{4} \div \dfrac{9}{4}$

⑭ $\dfrac{6}{8} \div \dfrac{3}{6}$

⑮ $\dfrac{8}{4} \div \dfrac{7}{9}$

⑯ $\dfrac{6}{9} \div \dfrac{8}{5}$

⑰ $\dfrac{9}{6} \div \dfrac{7}{3}$

⑱ $\dfrac{4}{9} \div \dfrac{2}{4}$

⑲ $\dfrac{5}{2} \div \dfrac{3}{6}$

⑳ $\dfrac{8}{3} \div \dfrac{9}{6}$

㉑ $\dfrac{6}{9} \div \dfrac{8}{4}$

㉒ $\dfrac{3}{7} \div \dfrac{8}{2}$

㉓ $\dfrac{7}{9} \div \dfrac{8}{5}$

㉔ $\dfrac{8}{7} \div \dfrac{5}{6}$

© Libro Studio LLC 2020

Name: _____

Score:

① $\dfrac{3}{3} \div \dfrac{5}{2}$

② $5 \div \dfrac{7}{4}$

③ $2 \div \dfrac{3}{6}$

④ $\dfrac{5}{9} \div \dfrac{6}{4}$

⑤ $\dfrac{6}{2} \div 2$

⑥ $\dfrac{8}{2} \div \dfrac{5}{4}$

⑦ $\dfrac{9}{4} \div \dfrac{2}{8}$

⑧ $\dfrac{3}{8} \div \dfrac{6}{4}$

⑨ $\dfrac{10}{8} \div \dfrac{6}{4}$

⑩ $\dfrac{5}{4} \div \dfrac{7}{5}$

⑪ $10 \div \dfrac{3}{5}$

⑫ $\dfrac{2}{9} \div 6$

⑬ $\dfrac{6}{2} \div \dfrac{3}{9}$

⑭ $8 \div \dfrac{4}{3}$

⑮ $\dfrac{9}{2} \div \dfrac{3}{10}$

⑯ $\dfrac{8}{4} \div 6$

⑰ $\dfrac{2}{9} \div \dfrac{3}{8}$

⑱ $\dfrac{8}{9} \div \dfrac{3}{4}$

⑲ $\dfrac{6}{4} \div \dfrac{10}{5}$

⑳ $\dfrac{6}{2} \div \dfrac{3}{4}$

㉑ $\dfrac{5}{6} \div \dfrac{2}{4}$

㉒ $\dfrac{7}{2} \div \dfrac{10}{4}$

㉓ $9 \div \dfrac{5}{4}$

㉔ $\dfrac{5}{2} \div \dfrac{4}{9}$

© Libro Studio LLC 2020

Name: _____

Score:

① $\dfrac{7}{5} \div \dfrac{2}{4}$

② $\dfrac{8}{9} \div \dfrac{3}{6}$

③ $\dfrac{8}{6} \div 2$

④ $\dfrac{3}{4} \div \dfrac{3}{9}$

⑤ $5 \div \dfrac{5}{4}$

⑥ $\dfrac{9}{4} \div \dfrac{8}{2}$

⑦ $\dfrac{6}{3} \div 5$

⑧ $\dfrac{7}{2} \div \dfrac{8}{2}$

⑨ $\dfrac{6}{3} \div \dfrac{4}{7}$

⑩ $9 \div \dfrac{2}{4}$

⑪ $\dfrac{7}{2} \div \dfrac{3}{8}$

⑫ $\dfrac{3}{4} \div \dfrac{9}{2}$

⑬ $2 \div \dfrac{10}{4}$

⑭ $6 \div \dfrac{10}{9}$

⑮ $\dfrac{5}{2} \div \dfrac{3}{6}$

⑯ $\dfrac{3}{6} \div \dfrac{4}{2}$

⑰ $\dfrac{9}{2} \div \dfrac{3}{8}$

⑱ $6 \div \dfrac{8}{9}$

⑲ $2 \div \dfrac{3}{5}$

⑳ $4 \div \dfrac{9}{3}$

㉑ $\dfrac{5}{2} \div \dfrac{6}{4}$

㉒ $\dfrac{6}{4} \div \dfrac{8}{9}$

㉓ $\dfrac{5}{6} \div \dfrac{7}{4}$

㉔ $\dfrac{5}{4} \div \dfrac{3}{5}$

© Libro Studio LLC 2020

Name: _____

Score:

① $\dfrac{5}{2} \div \dfrac{6}{9}$

② $\dfrac{6}{9} \div \dfrac{3}{2}$

③ $3 \div \dfrac{3}{7}$

④ $5 \div \dfrac{8}{2}$

⑤ $\dfrac{6}{2} \div \dfrac{3}{5}$

⑥ $7 \div \dfrac{3}{5}$

⑦ $\dfrac{7}{6} \div 2$

⑧ $\dfrac{3}{9} \div \dfrac{3}{8}$

⑨ $5 \div \dfrac{2}{4}$

⑩ $\dfrac{6}{4} \div \dfrac{3}{5}$

⑪ $\dfrac{3}{2} \div \dfrac{3}{9}$

⑫ $\dfrac{4}{8} \div \dfrac{2}{4}$

⑬ $\dfrac{6}{2} \div \dfrac{8}{5}$

⑭ $2 \div \dfrac{8}{9}$

⑮ $6 \div \dfrac{8}{5}$

⑯ $\dfrac{3}{8} \div \dfrac{9}{10}$

⑰ $4 \div \dfrac{6}{2}$

⑱ $\dfrac{8}{9} \div 2$

⑲ $\dfrac{4}{7} \div 5$

⑳ $\dfrac{6}{2} \div \dfrac{4}{10}$

㉑ $\dfrac{9}{5} \div \dfrac{10}{4}$

㉒ $\dfrac{4}{6} \div \dfrac{10}{4}$

㉓ $\dfrac{3}{3} \div \dfrac{2}{5}$

㉔ $\dfrac{4}{4} \div \dfrac{9}{8}$

© Libro Studio LLC 2020

Day 86
Dividing Fractions

Name: _____

Score: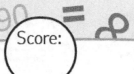

① $\dfrac{5}{3} \div \dfrac{3}{9}$

② $\dfrac{2}{6} \div \dfrac{3}{5}$

③ $3 \div \dfrac{3}{5}$

④ $\dfrac{3}{2} \div \dfrac{3}{5}$

⑤ $\dfrac{5}{4} \div 2$

⑥ $\dfrac{9}{3} \div \dfrac{3}{2}$

⑦ $6 \div \dfrac{2}{8}$

⑧ $\dfrac{7}{4} \div 2$

⑨ $\dfrac{9}{7} \div \dfrac{3}{8}$

⑩ $4 \div \dfrac{8}{3}$

⑪ $\dfrac{9}{2} \div \dfrac{3}{5}$

⑫ $\dfrac{6}{4} \div \dfrac{9}{2}$

⑬ $3 \div \dfrac{2}{8}$

⑭ $\dfrac{10}{7} \div 7$

⑮ $6 \div \dfrac{2}{8}$

⑯ $\dfrac{3}{5} \div \dfrac{7}{6}$

⑰ $\dfrac{10}{9} \div \dfrac{3}{8}$

⑱ $\dfrac{5}{4} \div \dfrac{4}{6}$

⑲ $\dfrac{6}{2} \div 5$

⑳ $\dfrac{6}{2} \div \dfrac{3}{3}$

㉑ $\dfrac{6}{2} \div \dfrac{8}{9}$

㉒ $\dfrac{3}{9} \div \dfrac{3}{8}$

㉓ $3 \div \dfrac{8}{4}$

㉔ $6 \div \dfrac{3}{9}$

© Libro Studio LLC 2020

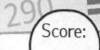

Name: _____

Score:

① $\dfrac{5}{4} \div 6$

② $\dfrac{9}{8} \div 5$

③ $\dfrac{2}{9} \div \dfrac{3}{3}$

④ $\dfrac{6}{8} \div \dfrac{9}{7}$

⑤ $\dfrac{3}{5} \div \dfrac{8}{4}$

⑥ $\dfrac{9}{4} \div \dfrac{3}{8}$

⑦ $6 \div \dfrac{2}{8}$

⑧ $3 \div \dfrac{8}{7}$

⑨ $\dfrac{3}{8} \div 4$

⑩ $\dfrac{9}{7} \div \dfrac{2}{3}$

⑪ $\dfrac{7}{2} \div \dfrac{3}{9}$

⑫ $\dfrac{8}{2} \div \dfrac{3}{7}$

⑬ $6 \div \dfrac{3}{8}$

⑭ $\dfrac{9}{8} \div \dfrac{3}{2}$

⑮ $\dfrac{5}{2} \div \dfrac{3}{6}$

⑯ $\dfrac{3}{4} \div \dfrac{3}{5}$

⑰ $2 \div \dfrac{3}{8}$

⑱ $\dfrac{9}{2} \div \dfrac{3}{5}$

⑲ $5 \div \dfrac{8}{4}$

⑳ $\dfrac{6}{2} \div \dfrac{6}{7}$

㉑ $6 \div \dfrac{3}{6}$

㉒ $\dfrac{2}{3} \div \dfrac{2}{8}$

㉓ $7 \div \dfrac{3}{5}$

㉔ $\dfrac{7}{5} \div \dfrac{6}{2}$

© Libro Studio LLC 2020

Day 88
Dividing Fractions

Name: _____

Score:

① $\dfrac{3}{9} \div \dfrac{2}{5}$

② $5 \div \dfrac{7}{4}$

③ $9 \div \dfrac{6}{8}$

④ $\dfrac{3}{8} \div 3$

⑤ $\dfrac{6}{4} \div \dfrac{2}{7}$

⑥ $\dfrac{8}{6} \div \dfrac{9}{2}$

⑦ $\dfrac{9}{7} \div \dfrac{3}{8}$

⑧ $\dfrac{6}{3} \div 2$

⑨ $\dfrac{6}{8} \div \dfrac{7}{5}$

⑩ $\dfrac{9}{10} \div \dfrac{4}{2}$

⑪ $\dfrac{8}{3} \div \dfrac{9}{6}$

⑫ $\dfrac{9}{8} \div \dfrac{8}{10}$

⑬ $7 \div \dfrac{2}{8}$

⑭ $\dfrac{9}{2} \div \dfrac{3}{3}$

⑮ $8 \div \dfrac{9}{8}$

⑯ $\dfrac{3}{4} \div \dfrac{9}{8}$

⑰ $5 \div \dfrac{7}{4}$

⑱ $2 \div \dfrac{9}{2}$

⑲ $8 \div \dfrac{5}{4}$

⑳ $9 \div \dfrac{6}{3}$

㉑ $\dfrac{5}{2} \div 8$

㉒ $\dfrac{4}{8} \div \dfrac{2}{5}$

㉓ $\dfrac{9}{3} \div \dfrac{2}{5}$

㉔ $\dfrac{4}{8} \div \dfrac{9}{7}$

© Libro Studio LLC 2020

1/4 % 5.3 × 3.107 290 = 8 7

Name: _____

Score:

① $\dfrac{4}{3} \div \dfrac{2}{5}$

② $5 \div \dfrac{6}{5}$

③ $\dfrac{4}{7} \div 8$

④ $\dfrac{9}{6} \div 2$

⑤ $\dfrac{3}{9} \div 2$

⑥ $\dfrac{10}{4} \div \dfrac{3}{10}$

⑦ $\dfrac{9}{8} \div \dfrac{2}{9}$

⑧ $\dfrac{7}{9} \div \dfrac{8}{4}$

⑨ $\dfrac{4}{8} \div \dfrac{10}{4}$

⑩ $\dfrac{2}{4} \div \dfrac{7}{9}$

⑪ $\dfrac{2}{4} \div \dfrac{5}{6}$

⑫ $\dfrac{2}{4} \div \dfrac{9}{2}$

⑬ $10 \div \dfrac{6}{5}$

⑭ $9 \div \dfrac{7}{5}$

⑮ $\dfrac{3}{9} \div \dfrac{4}{8}$

⑯ $\dfrac{6}{5} \div \dfrac{4}{3}$

⑰ $6 \div \dfrac{9}{5}$

⑱ $\dfrac{3}{7} \div \dfrac{6}{5}$

⑲ $\dfrac{3}{5} \div \dfrac{3}{6}$

⑳ $\dfrac{6}{4} \div \dfrac{9}{8}$

㉑ $\dfrac{4}{7} \div \dfrac{3}{5}$

㉒ $\dfrac{3}{4} \div \dfrac{3}{8}$

㉓ $5 \div \dfrac{7}{3}$

㉔ $\dfrac{2}{9} \div \dfrac{2}{6}$

© Libro Studio LLC 2020

Day 90
Dividing Fractions

Name: _____

Score:

① $\dfrac{5}{2} \div \dfrac{3}{3}$

② $\dfrac{9}{4} \div \dfrac{3}{6}$

③ $\dfrac{2}{2} \div \dfrac{7}{4}$

④ $8 \div \dfrac{2}{9}$

⑤ $9 \div \dfrac{4}{5}$

⑥ $\dfrac{4}{9} \div \dfrac{3}{8}$

⑦ $\dfrac{6}{3} \div 2$

⑧ $\dfrac{9}{5} \div 4$

⑨ $\dfrac{6}{10} \div 2$

⑩ $\dfrac{8}{2} \div 3$

⑪ $\dfrac{2}{8} \div \dfrac{10}{4}$

⑫ $\dfrac{9}{8} \div \dfrac{2}{8}$

⑬ $2 \div \dfrac{5}{7}$

⑭ $6 \div \dfrac{8}{9}$

⑮ $\dfrac{3}{10} \div \dfrac{2}{4}$

⑯ $\dfrac{2}{5} \div \dfrac{2}{4}$

⑰ $\dfrac{3}{4} \div \dfrac{9}{6}$

⑱ $8 \div \dfrac{7}{9}$

⑲ $\dfrac{7}{8} \div \dfrac{3}{9}$

⑳ $\dfrac{2}{9} \div \dfrac{8}{6}$

㉑ $\dfrac{8}{6} \div \dfrac{6}{7}$

㉒ $10 \div \dfrac{2}{4}$

㉓ $\dfrac{6}{5} \div 2$

㉔ $\dfrac{3}{4} \div \dfrac{3}{5}$

© Libro Studio LLC 2020

Name: _____

Score:

(1) Marsha earned an 85% on her science quiz. It was a 20-point quiz. How many points did Marsha earn?

(2) After this quiz is recorded, Marsha will have earned 235 points out of the possible 250 points for the class. What percent of the possible points has she earned?

(3) A disease is attacking the trees in a local park. Experts estimate that the park has 500 trees and ¼ of them are currently infected. How many trees is that?

(4) Experts believe that 80 of the 500 trees will not survive the disease. If true, what percent of the 500 trees will survive?

© Libro Studio LLC 2020

Name: _____

Score:

(1) A baseball player hits the ball 28% of the time he's up to bat. If he bats 150 times in a season, how many hits should he get?

(2) Of the 150 times the player is up to bat, he hits 12 homeruns. What percent of the time does he hit a homerun when up to bat?

(3) Laura buys a ticket for the baseball game. A ticket is normally 12 dollars, but Laura has a 10% off coupon. How much does her ticket cost after the coupon is applied?

(4) The baseball stadium seats 5000 people. Laura estimates that only 70% of the seats are filled. If true, how many seats are empty?

© Libro Studio LLC 2020

(1) A computer has 750 gigabytes of storage. 645 of these gigabytes are currently being used. What percentage of the storage space is still free to use?

(2) The two biggest file folders are 39.51 gigabytes and 25.87 gigabytes. How much space are these two folders using?

(3) It's decided that 165 gigabytes out of the 645 being used should be deleted. After they are deleted, what percentage of the 750 total gigabytes will be free to use?

(4) A new memory drive is purchased so that the computer now has 1,500 gigabytes of storage. What <u>fraction</u> of this new memory drive was the old 750 gigabyte drive capable of storing?

© Libro Studio LLC 2020

¼ % 5.3 ✗ 3.107 290 = 8

Name: _____

Score:

① Mark is buying new school cloths. The cloths he picks out are normally 160 dollars, but they are currently ¼ off their normal price. How much will Mark have to pay for these cloths?

② The shoes Mark buys normally cost 75 dollars, but he uses a 15% off coupon. How much did he pay for the shoes after the coupon was applied?

③ Mark needs to buy 30 dollars' worth of books for his classes. He is also charged a 6% sales tax on the purchase of these books. How much do the books cost after the tax is applied?

④ Mark finds a backpack that is normally 25$, but right now it's on sale for 3.78$ less than the normal price. What is the sale price for this backpack?

© Libro Studio LLC 2020

1. A pastry shop makes 3,000 doughnuts each day. Four fifths of these doughnuts are frosted. How many of the doughnuts are not frosted?

2. Chocolate is the most popular flavor. That's why 1,800 of the 3,000 doughnuts made are always chocolate. What percentage of the total is that?

3. Coconut sprinkles are not very popular, so only 4% of the doughnuts are made with coconut. How many of the 3,000 is that?

4. The owner of the pastry shop decides to have a special sale. He thinks he will sell more because of the sale, so he decides to make 4,800 doughnuts this day. What percent increase is this from the normal 3,000 doughnuts?

© Libro Studio LLC 2020

1. Jenny puts 2,000 dollars in the bank. The bank agrees to pay her 3% interest each year. How much money does her money earn after a year?

2. Ben borrows 6,000 dollars from the bank to buy a car. The bank charges him 5% interest each year on this loan. How much interest will Ben need to pay after a year?

3. Kevin's parents want to borrow 50,000 dollars to buy a house. The first bank they talk to wants to charge them 3% interest for the loan. The second bank they talk to wants to charge 4% interest each year. How much money will his parents save after a year if they decide to borrow from the first bank?

4. Jacob has 9,000 dollars in a bank that pays him 0.5% interest. He decides to move his money to a bank that will pay him 2% interest. How much more money will his 9,000 dollars earn each year because of the move?

© Libro Studio LLC 2020

1/4 % 5.3 x 3.107 290 = 8 ^

Name: _____

Score:

Use the following information to answer each question:

A school with 400 students had an election for student president. The results have been posted on this graph.

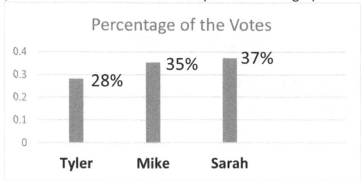

Percentage of the Votes

28%   35%   37%

Tyler   Mike   Sarah

① How many votes did Tyler receive?

② How many votes did Mike receive?

③ How many votes did Sarah receive?

④ How many of Tyler's votes would Mike have needed to beat Sarah?

© Libro Studio LLC 2020

Name: _____

Score:

① Anna orders 24 pizza's for her party. A third of the pizzas are pepperoni. How many pizza's is that?

② The pizzas cost Anna 300 dollars. She wants to give the pizza delivery driver a 12% tip. How much should she give the driver?

③ Anna buys 25 large bottles of soda for the party too. This many soda's normally cost 25 dollars, but she gets them on sale for 5% off. How much money did she save?

④ Anna's guests only eat ¾ of the 24 pizza's she ordered. How many pizza's are left?

© Libro Studio LLC 2020

① John is in an archery competition. He shoots 300 arrows and hits the bullseye 228 times. What percentage of his shots hit the bullseye?

② Crystal is also in the archery competition. 84% of her 300 arrows hit the bullseye. How many bullseyes did she hit?

③ The winner of the archery competition hit the bullseye every time they shot an arrow. What percentage of the winner's arrows hit the bullseye?

④ Kyle took last place in the competition. 7% of his arrows didn't even hit the target. How many of his 300 arrows missed the target?

© Libro Studio LLC 2020

Name: _____

Score:

① A king had 25,000 gold coins but spent a fifth of them to build a new castle. How much did the new castle cost?

② The king planned to spend 500 gold coins on crocodiles for the new moat, but he was able to buy some for 35% less than that. How much did he pay for the crocodiles?

③ The new castle will have a tower with one and a half times more stories than the old castle's tower. If the old tower was 6 stories high, how many stories will the new tower have?

④ The dining hall in the old castle could seat 200 guests. The new dining hall can seat 350% more guests than the old one. How many guests can the new dining hall seat?

© Libro Studio LLC 2020

Answers

Day 1:
1) D 2) B 3) D 4) A
5) 0.77 6) 46% 7) 0.035 8) 671%
9) 0.16 10) 8% 11) 1.49 12) 9.2%
13) 0.28 14) 10% 15) 0.9 16) 0.5%

Day 2:
1) 1 2) 50% 3) 0.33$\overline{3}$ 4) 66.$\overline{6}$%
5) 0.25 6) 50% 7) $\frac{3}{4}$ 8) 20%
9) $\frac{2}{5}$ 10) 0.6 11) $\frac{4}{5}$ 12) 12.5%
13) 0.1 14) 5% 15) 0.01

Day 3:
1) B 2) C 3) A 4) B
5) D 6) C 7) A 8) C
9) 0.382 10) 2360% 11) 0.47 12) 0.35%
13) 0.116 14) 80% 15) 0.078 16) 64.1%
17) 4.61 18) 335% 19) 0.59 20) 2.3%

Day 4:
1) H 2) E 3) A 4) I
5) D 6) C 7) J 8) F
9) B 10) G 11) D 12) A
13) D 14) B

Day 5:
1) 100% 2) 0.5 3) 33.$\overline{3}$% 4) $\frac{2}{3}$
5) $\frac{1}{4}$ 6) 0.5 7) 75% 8) 0.2
9) 40% 10) $\frac{3}{5}$ 11) 0.8 12) 0.125
13) $\frac{1}{10}$ 14) 0.05 15) $\frac{1}{100}$

Day 6:
1) B 2) C 3) A 4) D
5) D 6) C 7) A 8) D
9) 0.19 10) 725% 11) 0.80 12) 4%
13) 0.002 14) 99% 15) 0.503 16) 400%
17) 2.76 18) 10.1% 19) 0.09 20) 65%

Day 7:
1) C 2) A 3) I 4) F
5) J 6) B 7) H 8) G
9) D 10) E 11) A 12) A
13) C 14) B

Day 8:
1) 3 2) 4% 3) 0.12 4) 2%
5) 0.06 6) 82% 7) $\frac{3}{4}$ 8)) $\frac{1}{5}$
9) $\frac{1}{4}$ 10) $\frac{1}{8}$ 11) $\frac{1}{3}$ 12) $\frac{2}{3}$
13) $\frac{1}{10}$ 14) $\frac{7}{10}$ 15) $\frac{1}{100}$

Day 9:
1) C 2) B 3) C 4) D
5) D 6) B 7) D 8) D
9) 0.006 10) 370% 11) 5 12) 0.9%
13) 0.02 14) 13% 15) 0.178 16) 62.8%
17) 0.64 18) 405% 19) 0.203 20) 134.7%

Day 10:
1) F 2) I 3) E 4) B
5) J 6) A 7) D 8) H
9) G 10) C 11) B 12) C
13) A 14) B

Day 11:
1) 0.23 2) $\frac{3}{4}$ 3) $\frac{3}{20}$ 4) 66.$\overline{6}$%
5) $\frac{1}{20}$ 6) 50% 7) 0.04 8) 50%
9) 0.33$\overline{3}$ 10) 0.6 11) $\frac{4}{5}$ 12) 12.5%
13) 0.25 14) $\frac{1}{5}$ 15) 0.02

Day 12:
1) A 2) D 3) C 4) B
5) D 6) B 7) A 8) A
9) 0.54 10) 0.7% 11) 0.121 12) 8.5%
13) 1.37 14) 612% 15) 0.022 16) 95.3%
17) 0.459 18) 30% 19) 0.003 20) 150%

Day 13:
1) B 2) F 3) C 4) A
5) J 6) H 7) D 8) I
9) I 10) G 11) B 12) B
13) D 14) A

Day 14:
1) 20% 2) 5% 3) 0.33$\overline{3}$ 4) $\frac{1}{100}$
5) 0.25 6) $\frac{3}{20}$ 7) $\frac{3}{4}$ 8) 50%
9) $\frac{2}{3}$ 10) 0.92 11) $\frac{1}{10}$ 12) 12.5%
13) 0.1 14) 0.1% 15) 0.34

Day 15:
1) 46.37 2) 12.28 3) 7.1 4) 99.78
5) 20.16 6) 1.64 7) 80.5 8) 1.371
9) 7.45 10) 1.43 11) 13.219 12) 58.7
13) 52.644 14) 0.39 15) 1.3 16) 0.29

Day 16:
1) 10.28 2) 11.3 3) 8.17 4) 10.7
5) 9.28 6) 5.29 7) 40.42 8) 11.03
9) 66.83 10) 17.58 11) 13.43 12) 9.65
13) 5.91 14) 1.22 15) 72.57 16) 0.78
17) 7.68 18) 0.31 19) 2.11 20) 2.88
21) 4.67 22) 1.51 23) 7.39 24) 2.41

Day 17:
1) 14.87 2) 6.17 3) 5.96 4) 85.74
5) 4.72 6) 6.03 7) 11.79 8) 26.29
9) 12.14 10) 16.41 11) 13.56 12) 9.29
13) 65.27 14) 7.3 15) 3.71 16) 3
17) 2.09 18) 3.68 19) 6.45 20) 1
21) 0.1 22) 5.78 23) 2.28 24) 7.04

Day 18:
1) 6.63 2) 4.24 3) 10.31 4) 10.56
5) 8.88 6) 14.53 7) 34.6 8) 14.22
9) 82.48 10) 5.51 11) 14.1 12) 81.8
13) 0.13 14) 27.37 15) 6.24 16) 40.9
17) 0.22 18) 2.81 19) 0.72 20) 18.14
21) 3.07 22) 4.01 23) 0.52 24) 0.08

Day 19:
1) 11.63 2) 61.09 3) 8.82 4) 7.2
5) 1.45 6) 7.47 7) 18.44 8) 5.82
9) 13.71 10) 2.62 11) 6.22 12) 10.18
13) 0.35 14) 7.38 15) 5.8 16) 0.34
17) 1.48 18) 7.57 19) 47.77 20) 0.99
21) 0.04 22) 0.27 23) 0.01 24) 25.33

Day 20:
1) 14.46 2) 82.12 3) 4.45 4) 3.51
5) 11.23 6) 9.41 7) 13.38 8) 9.5
9) 4.04 10) 15.85 11) 6.91 12) 28.23
13) 10.47 14) 1.01 15) 3.17 16) 5.91
17) 0.99 18) 3.98 19) 12.79 20) 0.17
21) 1.27 22) 0.57 23) 2.54 24) 6

Day 21:
1) 9.88 2) 11.47 3) 2.3 4) 49.14
5) 3.1 6) 13.31 7) 9.41 8) 18.07
9) 2.42 10) 39.22 11) 4.31 12) 20.56
13) 0.16 14) 33.73 15) 0.25 16) 3.96
17) 4.59 18) 2.36 19) 1.69 20) 0.52
21) 2.3 22) 9.08 23) 34.86 24) 1.73

Day 22:
1) 19.31 2) 7.9 3) 56.93 4) 10.89
5) 8.93 6) 14.55 7) 18.65 8) 17.97
9) 12.46 10) 4.14 11) 68.49 12) 15.73
13) 5.74 14) 0.27 15) 9.96 16) 0.79
17) 3.66 18) 3.08 19) 3.74 20) 3.87
21) 7.66 22) 2.38 23) 0.43 24) 2.94

Day 23:
1) 8.87 2) 13.31 3) 8.45 4) 5.48
5) 64.57 6) 40.32 7) 8.78 8) 7.29
9) 8.85 10) 7.89 11) 3.35 12) 29.81
13) 1.58 14) 5.45 15) 7.14 16) 0.75
17) 1.57 18) 3.27 19) 0.07 20) 2.32
21) 3.32 22) 0.36 23) 9.95 24) 0.96

Day 24:
1) 6.8 2) 13.02 3) 18.35 4) 12.03
5) 19.02 6) 10.51 7) 10.25 8) 12.41
9) 7.45 10) 13.78 11) 11.32 12) 8.41
13) 1.68 14) 4.5 15) 3.92 16) 0.77
17) 4.93 18) 5.06 19) 3.16 20) 0.16
21) 2 22) 1.35 23) 4.83 24) 1.02

Day 25:
1) 16.95 2) 7.57 3) 16.23 4) 22.44
5) 7.51 6) 7.33 7) 12.65 8) 12.21
9) 12.71 10) 1.11 11) 90.2 12) 17.68
13) 2.06 14) 6.55 15) 6.26 16) 9.29
17) 1.52 18) 1.1 19) 4.87 20) 0.12
21) 2.54 22) 4.91 23) 7.08 24) 0.29

Day 26:
1) 11.47 2) 9.82 3) 30.63 4) 7.53
5) 7.42 6) 11.75 7) 9.55 8) 14.78
9) 4.16 10) 13.42 11) 75.48 12) 17.5
13) 4.96 14) 0 15) 1.88 16) 2.24
17) 25.6 18) 2.35 19) 26.39 20) 0.26
21) 3.06 22) 6.92 23) 0.44 24) 5.97

Day 27:
1) 54.42 2) 6.67 3) 10.06 4) 3.56
5) 16.55 6) 13.86 7) 10.54 8) 82.82
9) 44.54 10) 0.86 11) 14.69 12) 6.8
13) 5.21 14) 7.08 15) 2.27 16) 10.38
17) 81.09 18) 0.18 19) 2.93 20) 8.93
21) 5.5 22) 2.29 23) 0.2 24) 3.82

Day 28:
1) 14.48 2) 11.28 3) 8 4) 7.38
5) 5.82 6) 15.9 7) 5.33 8) 20.03
9) 16.04 10) 17.8 11) 13.31 12) 9.43
13) 12.8 14) 0.25 15) 12.17 16) 2.79
17) 0.68 18) 4.92 19) 3.74 20) 3.23
21) 17.1 22) 4.17 23) 1.5 24) 51.39

© Libro Studio LLC 2020

Answers

Day 29:
1) 0.91 2) 4.32 3) 5.84 4) 9.26
5) 9.49 6) 22.1 7) 4.6 8) 43.25
9) 3.08 10) 4.48 11) 14.37 12) 65.8
13) 6.41 14) 7.37 15) 4.42 16) 4.4
17) 4.82 18) 3.02 19) 33.77 20) 7.65
21) 3.52 22) 0.13 23) 5.87 24) 2.92

Day 30:
1) 17.08 2) 10.42 3) 16.5 4) 4.47
5) 8.31 6) 13.84 7) 3.38 8) 8.61
9) 9.97 10) 9.39 11) 13.46 12) 4.83
13) 0.06 14) 4.91 15) 3.97 16) 72.9
17) 4.07 18) 2.66 19) 1.29 20) 9.2
21) 4.87 22) 5.24 23) 0.09 24) 2.3

Day 31:
1) 65.7 2) 1500 3) 5,260 4) 82
5) 1.32 6) 380 7) 4,240 8) 975.7
9) 970.8 10) 6,100 11) 74,000 12) 280.1
13) 320 14) 4,405 15) 0.5 16) 7,240

Day 32:
1) 960 2) 500 3) 2.5 4) 1,500
5) 62,800 6) 43 7) 0.5 8) 831
9) 9,300 10) 22.08 11) 2,270 12) 250
13) 1,160 14) 35.2 15) 13,700 16) 72.3
17) 83,000 18) 621 19) 200 20) 3
21) 7.6 22) 0.05 23) 971 24) 8,100

Day 33:
1) 1.971 2) 13.503 3) 25.774 4) 46.74
5) 871.2 6) 1.8886 7) 110.24 8) 78.056
9) 33.10428 10) 18.422 11) 37 12) 25.209
13) 0.5152 14) 114.53 15) 0.39 16) 474.22

Day 34:
1) 75 2) 75 3) 36.88 4) 12.083
5) 60.59 6) 91.6 7) 2.4 8) 2
9) 36.48 10) 29.1084 11) 3 12) 116.28
13) 3.7 14) 47.088 15) 85.86 16) 67.575
17) 5.751 18) 870 19) 217.2 20) 7.7
21) 11.3286 22) 3.2643 23) 2.64 24) 50.325

Day 35:
1) 24.576 2) 20 3) 2 4) 3
5) 48.356 6) 36.98 7) 0.4505 8) 30.0822
9) 28.83 10) 330 11) 63.56 12) 12.5
13) 107.3 14) 21.472 15) 53.841 16) 31.812
17) 47.393 18) 55.89 19) 200 20) 30
21) 8.74 22) 126 23) 52.434 24) 26.73

Day 36:
1) 29.3344 2) 18.972 3) 23.0464 4) 3.6576
5) 9.964 6) 16.3285 7) 19.224 8) 54.219
9) 55.38 10) 201.552 11) 22.4016 12) 21.2
13) 4,550 14) 28.3856 15) 113.634 16) 14.31
17) 26.8932 18) 53.424 19) 35.88 20) 18.333
21) 12.2 22) 20.336 23) 15.486 24) 1.5748

Day 37:
1) 76.32 2) 51.086 3) 3.6408 4) 6.46
5) 91.2 6) 614.94 7) 17.0142 8) 15.9488
9) 9.471 10) 11.5388 11) 44.268 12) 114.45
13) 17.3166 14) 6.7404 15) 1.659 16) 31.93
17) 32.016 18) 5.046 19) 5.2197 20) 87.6
21) 1.6996 22) 247 23) 4.0602 24) 81.76

Day 38:
1) 11.0986 2) 12.62 3) 15.718 4) 57.66
5) 0.3786 6) 64.064 7) 0.594 8) 623
9) 258.99 10) 63.96 11) 118.736 12) 36.423
13) 35 14) 68.15 15) 36.1 16) 8.253
17) 75.9 18) 52.332 19) 16 20) 109.12
21) 15.2 22) 20.46 23) 0.02 24) 54.63

Day 39:
1) 2.044 2) 15 3) 0.233 4) 1
5) 30 6) 125 7) 88.14 8) 192
9) 56 10) 1.625 11) 4.44 12) 3.5
13) 0.016 14) 93 15) 20 16) 1,350
17) 4.875 18) 90 19) 1 20) 6
21) 45.212 22) 26.4 23) 243 24) 15

Day 40:
1) 4.8 2) 20 3) 9.825 4) 60
5) 70 6) 300 7) 125 8) 66
9) 8.36 10) 1.5 11) 4.656 12) 2.8
13) 20 14) 0.465 15) 9 16) 420
17) 24.32 18) 4.2 19) 52 20) 18
21) 4.488 22) 2 23) 440 24) 36

Day 41:
1) 0.408 2) 2.972 3) 0.0206 4) 1.596
5) 0.014 6) 0.007 7) 3.105 8) 0.0047
9) 0.176 10) 11.65 11) 0.0022 12) 0.00007
13) 0.2096 14) 0.0032 15) 18.55 16) 0.492

Day 42:
1) 2.796 2) 1.6116 3) 0.04564 4) 10.4
5) 20.448 6) 0.13692 7) 0.058 8) 0.465
9) 8.132 10) 32.7 11) 3.2571 12) 0.5096
13) 0.502 14) 5.852 15) 0.0017 16) 0.788
17) 0.1858 18) 1.219 19) 6.941 20) 0.017
21) 41.04 22) 1.774 23) 0.0426 24) 0.0209

Day 43:
1) 0.3136 2) 12.932 3) 0.4135 4) 2.056
5) 0.153 6) 27.4 7) 0.0636 8) 1.862
9) 1.2 10) 0.05 11) 0.902 12) 0.1166
13) 0.558 14) 0.0287 15) 12.474 16) 0.06552
17) 0.04368 18) 0.931 19) 0.4446 20) 9.4
21) 52.65 22) 1.407 23) 8.991 24) 0.07781

Day 44:
1) 19 2) 59 3) 6.75 4) 76
5) 15.6 6) 9.3 7) 0.428 8) 3.25
9) 35.8 10) 0.8 11) 1.26 12) 92
13) 1.21 14) 28 15) 4.76 16) 7.3

Day 45:
1) 6 2) 12.11 3) 7.8 4) 2
5) 33 6) 2 7) 12 8) 9.44
9) 7 10) 65 11) 2.12 12) 3.45
13) 8.21 14) 230 15) 3.41 16) 23.1
17) 1.11 18) 6.14 19) 9.27 20) 7.21
21) 63 22) 12.3 23) 3.2 24) 9.13

Day 46:
1) 3.09 2) 2.78 3) 2.91 4) 2.93
5) 2.74 6) 2.87 7) 2.79 8) 2.75
9) 3 10) 2.91 11) 8 12) 18
13) 49 14) 2 15) 6.11 16) 46
17) 18 18) 11 19) 14 20) 15
21) 10 22) 3.14 23) 8.58 24) 2.41

Day 47:
1) 1 2) 9 3) 8 4) 7
5) 5.77 6) 2 7) 4 8) 10
9) 6 10) 3 11) 2.83 12) 6.78
13) 2.93 14) 2.72 15) 6.74 16) 2.99
17) 1.01 18) 8 19) 5 20) 12
21) 20 22) 18 23) 0.34 24) 0.96

Day 48:
1) 26 2) 12 3) 16 4) 27
5) 2.57 6) 28 7) 21 8) 13
9) 2.86 10) 2.78 11) 2.73 12) 2.91
13) 2.86 14) 2.79 15) 7.94 16) 2.89
17) 3.07 18) 2.92 19) 12 20) 25
21) 53 22) 0.23 23) 2.1 24) 8

Day 49:
1) 14 2) 2.1 3) 0.4 4) 28
5) 33 6) 5 7) 17 8) 3
9) 24 10) 70 11) 29 12) 19
13) 60 14) 82 15) 4 16) 43
17) 61 18) 2.52 19) 0.69 20) 6
21) 0.28 22) 3 23) 67 24) 8.12

Day 50:
1) 5.263 2) 63 3) 11 4) 2.857
5) 7.96 6) 7.5 7) 14 8) 8.2
9) 3 10) 71 11) 3 12) 72
13) 59 14) 74 15) 54 16) 0.74
17) 74 18) 21 19) 51 20) 53
21) 75 22) 62 23) 7 24) 68

Day 51:
1) $\frac{1}{2}$ 2) $\frac{1}{4}$ 3) $\frac{1}{4}$ 4) $\frac{1}{9}$

5) $1\frac{1}{2}$ 6) $4\frac{2}{5}$ 7) $1\frac{1}{4}$ 8) 7

9) $\frac{1}{10}$ 10) $\frac{1}{6}$ 11) $\frac{1}{24}$ 12) $\frac{1}{16}$

13) $8\frac{2}{5}$ 14) $3\frac{1}{6}$ 15) $2\frac{7}{9}$ 16) $1\frac{1}{6}$

Day 52:
1) $2\frac{1}{2}$ 2) $\frac{1}{3}$ 3) $\frac{2}{5}$ 4) $1\frac{1}{3}$

5) $\frac{6}{25}$ 6) $4\frac{1}{2}$ 7) $\frac{1}{2}$ 8) $\frac{1}{3}$

9) $\frac{1}{7}$ 10) $4\frac{1}{2}$ 11) $4\frac{2}{3}$ 12) $\frac{1}{6}$

13) $\frac{2}{9}$ 14) $\frac{5}{21}$ 15) $2\frac{1}{4}$ 16) $\frac{4}{13}$

17) $3\frac{2}{5}$ 18) $\frac{4}{17}$ 19) $\frac{7}{25}$ 20) $6\frac{1}{9}$

21) $3\frac{3}{7}$ 22) $\frac{1}{5}$ 23) $\frac{2}{13}$ 24) $\frac{2}{5}$

© Libro Studio LLC 2020

Answers

Day 53:
1) $1\frac{1}{2}$ 2) $\frac{2}{9}$ 3) $1\frac{5}{6}$ 4) $\frac{1}{45}$

5) $\frac{3}{4}$ 6) $\frac{3}{7}$ 7) $\frac{3}{14}$ 8) $\frac{5}{9}$

9) $25\frac{1}{2}$ 10) $\frac{1}{10}$ 11) $5\frac{3}{7}$ 12) $\frac{5}{18}$

13) $\frac{4}{9}$ 14) $\frac{3}{14}$ 15) $1\frac{2}{5}$ 16) $1\frac{4}{5}$

17) $\frac{1}{28}$ 18) $2\frac{3}{5}$ 19) $\frac{2}{5}$ 20) $\frac{1}{5}$

21) $1\frac{1}{4}$ 22) $8\frac{1}{3}$ 23) $\frac{4}{11}$ 24) $3\frac{4}{5}$

Day 54:
1) $\frac{8}{9}$ 2) $\frac{1}{20}$ 3) $\frac{1}{6}$ 4) $4\frac{2}{3}$

5) $1\frac{1}{2}$ 6) $\frac{1}{12}$ 7) 3 8) $27\frac{1}{3}$

9) $1\frac{2}{3}$ 10) $4\frac{4}{7}$ 11) $3\frac{1}{4}$ 12) $5\frac{1}{3}$

13) $\frac{4}{9}$ 14) $2\frac{8}{25}$ 15) $\frac{3}{5}$ 16) $\frac{2}{7}$

17) $2\frac{5}{7}$ 18) $\frac{1}{6}$ 19) $\frac{1}{8}$ 20) $3\frac{1}{3}$

21) $5\frac{1}{4}$ 22) $\frac{2}{9}$ 23) $1\frac{1}{4}$ 24) $\frac{2}{3}$

Day 55:
1) $\frac{1}{2}$ 2) $2\frac{1}{4}$ 3) $\frac{1}{4}$ 4) $\frac{1}{10}$

5) $1\frac{6}{7}$ 6) $2\frac{1}{2}$ 7) $\frac{1}{5}$ 8) $\frac{2}{3}$

9) $\frac{4}{13}$ 10) $\frac{5}{6}$ 11) $2\frac{1}{3}$ 12) $\frac{3}{11}$

13) 7 14) $8\frac{2}{5}$ 15) $5\frac{6}{7}$ 16) $1\frac{8}{9}$

17) $9\frac{1}{3}$ 18) $\frac{1}{5}$ 19) $\frac{1}{24}$ 20) $2\frac{1}{2}$

21) 5 22) $5\frac{1}{2}$ 23) $2\frac{3}{5}$ 24) $\frac{1}{3}$

Day 56:
1) $12\frac{6}{25}$ 2) $4\frac{1}{2}$ 3) $\frac{1}{8}$ 4) $\frac{6}{7}$

5) $\frac{1}{13}$ 6) $\frac{4}{5}$ 7) $\frac{4}{7}$ 8) $\frac{2}{7}$

9) $\frac{3}{50}$ 10) $3\frac{9}{25}$ 11) $\frac{3}{8}$ 12) $\frac{1}{14}$

13) $3\frac{1}{4}$ 14) $\frac{1}{33}$ 15) $5\frac{1}{6}$ 16) $\frac{5}{7}$

17) $5\frac{8}{9}$ 18) $\frac{1}{3}$ 19) $6\frac{4}{5}$ 20) $2\frac{1}{2}$

21) $2\frac{4}{7}$ 22) $\frac{3}{5}$ 23) $\frac{2}{11}$ 24) $3\frac{1}{8}$

Day 57:
1) $1\frac{2}{15}$ 2) $\frac{7}{8}$ 3) $\frac{9}{10}$ 4) $1\frac{1}{3}$

5) $1\frac{7}{18}$ 6) $\frac{14}{15}$ 7) $\frac{17}{30}$ 8) $\frac{7}{9}$

9) $\frac{13}{20}$ 10) $\frac{1}{21}$ 11) $\frac{13}{24}$ 12) $\frac{9}{28}$

13) $\frac{1}{6}$ 14) $\frac{11}{36}$ 15) $\frac{1}{10}$ 16) $\frac{1}{8}$

Day 58:
1) $1\frac{20}{63}$ 2) $4\frac{2}{9}$ 3) $\frac{11}{15}$ 4) $5\frac{3}{10}$

5) $1\frac{3}{7}$ 6) $1\frac{5}{8}$ 7) $2\frac{3}{4}$ 8) $2\frac{1}{2}$

9) $2\frac{20}{21}$ 10) $\frac{13}{14}$ 11) $1\frac{5}{28}$ 12) $\frac{13}{18}$

13) $\frac{1}{12}$ 14) $\frac{38}{63}$ 15) $\frac{9}{10}$ 16) $\frac{1}{7}$

17) $1\frac{2}{3}$ 18) $\frac{3}{4}$ 19) $\frac{31}{72}$ 20) $\frac{5}{6}$

21) $\frac{5}{14}$ 22) $\frac{1}{5}$ 23) $\frac{1}{4}$ 24) $\frac{5}{21}$

Day 59:
1) $2\frac{1}{3}$ 2) $4\frac{3}{4}$ 3) $2\frac{1}{2}$ 4) $3\frac{3}{7}$

5) $3\frac{1}{4}$ 6) $3\frac{7}{12}$ 7) 3 8) 3

9) $3\frac{13}{15}$ 10) $3\frac{5}{12}$ 11) $1\frac{11}{12}$ 12) $2\frac{1}{3}$

13) $\frac{1}{10}$ 14) $\frac{2}{3}$ 15) $\frac{5}{8}$ 16) $\frac{23}{99}$

17) $\frac{1}{4}$ 18) $\frac{1}{6}$ 19) $\frac{1}{3}$ 20) $\frac{3}{5}$

21) $\frac{25}{56}$ 22) $\frac{4}{5}$ 23) $\frac{11}{24}$ 24) $\frac{1}{12}$

Day 60:
1) $2\frac{3}{4}$ 2) $2\frac{9}{10}$ 3) $2\frac{7}{12}$ 4) $1\frac{5}{6}$

5) $2\frac{1}{2}$ 6) $1\frac{13}{18}$ 7) $1\frac{1}{12}$ 8) $1\frac{9}{14}$

9) $2\frac{1}{2}$ 10) $2\frac{2}{21}$ 11) $3\frac{3}{4}$ 12) $2\frac{1}{2}$

13) $\frac{1}{6}$ 14) $\frac{1}{10}$ 15) $\frac{3}{4}$ 16) $\frac{15}{28}$

17) $\frac{1}{9}$ 18) $\frac{23}{42}$ 19) $\frac{1}{8}$ 20) $\frac{7}{10}$

21) $1\frac{3}{10}$ 22) $\frac{7}{12}$ 23) $\frac{1}{14}$ 24) $\frac{1}{2}$

Day 61:
1) $3\frac{1}{3}$ 2) $1\frac{1}{2}$ 3) $3\frac{2}{5}$ 4) $1\frac{19}{21}$

5) $1\frac{32}{45}$ 6) $3\frac{1}{20}$ 7) $\frac{17}{18}$ 8) $2\frac{4}{15}$

9) $2\frac{1}{5}$ 10) $2\frac{1}{4}$ 11) 2 12) $3\frac{3}{10}$

13) $\frac{59}{84}$ 14) $\frac{3}{4}$ 15) $\frac{1}{20}$ 16) $\frac{8}{63}$

17) $\frac{1}{2}$ 18) $\frac{5}{72}$ 19) $\frac{1}{4}$ 20) $\frac{9}{10}$

21) $\frac{9}{14}$ 22) $\frac{1}{5}$ 23) $\frac{3}{5}$ 24) $\frac{20}{63}$

Day 62:
1) $1\frac{2}{3}$ 2) $2\frac{1}{4}$ 3) $1\frac{11}{15}$ 4) $2\frac{7}{20}$

5) $1\frac{1}{2}$ 6) 1 7) $2\frac{3}{5}$ 8) $2\frac{1}{2}$

9) $2\frac{1}{4}$ 10) $1\frac{1}{6}$ 11) $1\frac{13}{14}$ 12) $2\frac{1}{3}$

13) $\frac{19}{42}$ 14) $\frac{3}{10}$ 15) $\frac{1}{20}$ 16) $2\frac{1}{2}$

17) $\frac{1}{10}$ 18) $\frac{1}{3}$ 19) $\frac{22}{63}$ 20) $\frac{1}{14}$

21) $\frac{7}{24}$ 22) $\frac{17}{42}$ 23) $\frac{1}{4}$ 24) $\frac{12}{35}$

Day 63:
1) $\frac{35}{36}$ 2) $2\frac{1}{35}$ 3) $2\frac{1}{5}$ 4) $1\frac{1}{2}$

5) 1 6) $2\frac{4}{5}$ 7) $2\frac{1}{4}$ 8) $2\frac{1}{18}$

9) $1\frac{3}{5}$ 10) 3 11) $1\frac{17}{45}$ 12) $2\frac{1}{2}$

13) $1\frac{3}{10}$ 14) $\frac{1}{15}$ 15) $\frac{11}{12}$ 16) $\frac{13}{24}$

17) $\frac{23}{24}$ 18) $\frac{25}{63}$ 19) $\frac{1}{12}$ 20) $\frac{3}{20}$

21) $\frac{1}{4}$ 22) $\frac{37}{40}$ 23) $\frac{1}{6}$ 24) $\frac{1}{2}$

Day 64:
1) $3\frac{1}{5}$ 2) $2\frac{3}{4}$ 3) $2\frac{7}{8}$ 4) $2\frac{11}{28}$

5) $1\frac{13}{14}$ 6) $4\frac{3}{4}$ 7) $2\frac{5}{8}$ 8) $\frac{16}{21}$

9) $3\frac{2}{9}$ 10) $\frac{5}{6}$ 11) $1\frac{9}{10}$ 12) $2\frac{1}{6}$

13) $\frac{1}{9}$ 14) $\frac{1}{20}$ 15) $\frac{2}{3}$ 16) $\frac{7}{22}$

17) $1\frac{1}{6}$ 18) $\frac{1}{12}$ 19) 0 20) $\frac{7}{10}$

21) $\frac{3}{8}$ 22) $\frac{1}{3}$ 23) $\frac{-7}{10}$ 24) $\frac{1}{6}$

© Libro Studio LLC 2020

Answers

Day 65:
1) $2\frac{13}{20}$ 2) $3\frac{1}{10}$ 3) $1\frac{20}{21}$ 4) $1\frac{19}{36}$

5) $2\frac{12}{35}$ 6) 3 7) $2\frac{13}{21}$ 8) $3\frac{3}{4}$

9) $2\frac{1}{8}$ 10) $1\frac{13}{28}$ 11) $2\frac{1}{6}$ 12) $2\frac{1}{7}$

13) $\frac{1}{2}$ 14) $\frac{11}{28}$ 15) $\frac{31}{36}$ 16) $\frac{5}{12}$

17) $\frac{44}{45}$ 18) $\frac{1}{3}$ 19) $\frac{17}{30}$ 20) $1\frac{4}{15}$

21) $\frac{5}{42}$ 22) $\frac{27}{28}$ 23) $\frac{1}{3}$ 24) $\frac{19}{35}$

Day 66:
1) $3\frac{1}{4}$ 2) $2\frac{11}{12}$ 3) $1\frac{1}{18}$ 4) $2\frac{1}{3}$

5) 2 6) $2\frac{1}{20}$ 7) $1\frac{2}{3}$ 8) $\frac{11}{12}$

9) $2\frac{7}{8}$ 10) $3\frac{1}{6}$ 11) 2 12) $1\frac{16}{21}$

13) $\frac{9}{14}$ 14) $\frac{1}{4}$ 15) $\frac{39}{56}$ 16) $\frac{3}{10}$

17) $\frac{1}{4}$ 18) $\frac{1}{2}$ 19) $\frac{8}{15}$ 20) $\frac{3}{35}$

21) $\frac{1}{5}$ 22) $\frac{1}{4}$ 23) $\frac{1}{4}$ 24) $\frac{19}{72}$

Day 67:
1) $2\frac{1}{2}$ 2) $1\frac{17}{21}$ 3) $2\frac{3}{4}$ 4) $\frac{3}{4}$

5) 2 6) $2\frac{1}{4}$ 7) $2\frac{7}{40}$ 8) $\frac{7}{9}$

9) $1\frac{13}{18}$ 10) $1\frac{19}{40}$ 11) $1\frac{47}{56}$ 12) $4\frac{3}{5}$

13) $\frac{4}{15}$ 14) $\frac{3}{5}$ 15) $\frac{1}{12}$ 16) $\frac{1}{10}$

17) $\frac{5}{7}$ 18) $\frac{1}{6}$ 19) $\frac{2}{7}$ 20) $\frac{25}{28}$

21) $\frac{1}{12}$ 22) $\frac{1}{28}$ 23) $\frac{11}{12}$ 24) $\frac{3}{20}$

Day 68:
1) $1\frac{7}{24}$ 2) $1\frac{1}{3}$ 3) $1\frac{5}{9}$ 4) $2\frac{29}{30}$

5) $1\frac{2}{9}$ 6) $1\frac{5}{12}$ 7) $1\frac{41}{42}$ 8) $1\frac{47}{56}$

9) $\frac{79}{92}$ 10) $2\frac{3}{10}$ 11) $3\frac{7}{8}$ 12) $1\frac{17}{21}$

13) $\frac{12}{35}$ 14) $\frac{1}{5}$ 15) $\frac{7}{24}$ 16) $\frac{1}{2}$

17) 1 18) $\frac{1}{4}$ 19) $\frac{2}{5}$ 20) $\frac{25}{28}$

21) $\frac{7}{36}$ 22) $\frac{9}{28}$ 23) $\frac{1}{18}$ 24) $\frac{29}{56}$

Day 69:
1) 2 2) $2\frac{5}{8}$ 3) $2\frac{9}{10}$ 4) $2\frac{7}{8}$

5) $2\frac{3}{4}$ 6) $1\frac{5}{9}$ 7) $3\frac{7}{18}$ 8) $2\frac{5}{12}$

9) $2\frac{1}{12}$ 10) $1\frac{11}{42}$ 11) $3\frac{3}{10}$ 12) $\frac{25}{36}$

13) $\frac{1}{5}$ 14) $1\frac{1}{4}$ 15) $\frac{47}{56}$ 16) $\frac{7}{36}$

17) $\frac{1}{15}$ 18) $\frac{33}{35}$ 19) $\frac{29}{63}$ 20) $\frac{3}{20}$

21) $\frac{3}{10}$ 22) $\frac{1}{3}$ 23) $\frac{13}{45}$ 24) $\frac{1}{3}$

Day 70:
1) $2\frac{1}{4}$ 2) $1\frac{11}{28}$ 3) $1\frac{9}{20}$ 4) $1\frac{5}{18}$

5) $2\frac{19}{24}$ 6) $1\frac{19}{28}$ 7) $1\frac{19}{21}$ 8) $2\frac{2}{63}$

9) $2\frac{8}{15}$ 10) $2\frac{7}{8}$ 11) $2\frac{7}{9}$ 12) $1\frac{20}{63}$

13) $\frac{3}{10}$ 14) $\frac{11}{12}$ 15) $\frac{2}{15}$ 16) $\frac{1}{40}$

17) $\frac{1}{4}$ 18) $\frac{39}{56}$ 19) $\frac{3}{7}$ 20) $\frac{13}{40}$

21) $\frac{1}{5}$ 22) $\frac{1}{12}$ 23) $\frac{7}{20}$ 24) $2\frac{1}{2}$

Day 71:
1) $\frac{18}{35}$ 2) $\frac{5}{16}$ 3) $\frac{12}{25}$ 4) $\frac{14}{27}$

5) $2\frac{1}{4}$ 6) $\frac{9}{28}$ 7) 2 8) $\frac{7}{32}$

9) $\frac{1}{9}$ 10) $\frac{1}{3}$ 11) $\frac{3}{16}$ 12) $\frac{5}{18}$

13) $\frac{3}{16}$ 14) $\frac{12}{35}$ 15) $\frac{1}{2}$ 16) $\frac{1}{4}$

Day 72:
1) $\frac{5}{18}$ 2) $1\frac{8}{27}$ 3) $1\frac{8}{27}$ 4) 6

5) $3\frac{3}{7}$ 6) 12 7) $\frac{1}{6}$ 8) $1\frac{1}{14}$

9) $1\frac{3}{7}$ 10) 24 11) $\frac{8}{21}$ 12) 2

13) $\frac{4}{9}$ 14) $3\frac{3}{7}$ 15) $1\frac{2}{3}$ 16) $1\frac{13}{32}$

17) $5\frac{5}{6}$ 18) $1\frac{1}{5}$ 19) 6 20) $13\frac{1}{2}$

21) $1\frac{11}{16}$ 22) $\frac{35}{36}$ 23) $5\frac{3}{5}$ 24) $\frac{9}{10}$

Day 73:
1) $\frac{7}{10}$ 2) $2\frac{2}{5}$ 3) $\frac{1}{3}$ 4) $1\frac{2}{3}$

5) $10\frac{1}{2}$ 6) $\frac{1}{7}$ 7) $\frac{3}{8}$ 8) $\frac{9}{20}$

9) $\frac{9}{40}$ 10) $7\frac{1}{2}$ 11) $\frac{5}{6}$ 12) 1

13) 1 14) 1 15) 1 16) $1\frac{5}{7}$

17) $1\frac{7}{8}$ 18) $\frac{1}{2}$ 19) $1\frac{1}{3}$ 20) $\frac{20}{21}$

21) $1\frac{11}{45}$ 22) $2\frac{2}{7}$ 23) 1 24) $\frac{5}{12}$

Day 74:
1) $1\frac{13}{35}$ 2) $1\frac{1}{3}$ 3) $1\frac{1}{8}$ 4) $\frac{5}{27}$

5) $2\frac{4}{7}$ 6) $\frac{1}{4}$ 7) $1\frac{13}{14}$ 8) $\frac{3}{5}$

9) $1\frac{13}{14}$ 10) $\frac{2}{3}$ 11) $1\frac{1}{2}$ 12) $6\frac{2}{5}$

13) $\frac{27}{56}$ 14) $\frac{35}{72}$ 15) $\frac{3}{4}$ 16) 3

17) $\frac{4}{25}$ 18) $\frac{4}{9}$ 19) $4\frac{2}{3}$ 20) 1

21) 7 22) $\frac{1}{2}$ 23) $2\frac{1}{4}$ 24) $\frac{1}{5}$

Day 75:
1) $5\frac{1}{4}$ 2) 4 3) $\frac{8}{25}$ 4) $\frac{2}{7}$

5) $\frac{2}{3}$ 6) $\frac{3}{5}$ 7) 6 8) 6

9) $\frac{1}{3}$ 10) $3\frac{3}{7}$ 11) 1 12) $2\frac{2}{5}$

13) $1\frac{1}{7}$ 14) $4\frac{1}{5}$ 15) $\frac{3}{8}$ 16) $3\frac{15}{16}$

17) $\frac{3}{4}$ 18) $1\frac{1}{2}$ 19) 3 20) $1\frac{1}{5}$

21) $1\frac{1}{2}$ 22) $\frac{1}{3}$ 23) $\frac{9}{10}$ 24) 2

Day 76:
1) $\frac{9}{20}$ 2) $1\frac{7}{20}$ 3) $\frac{9}{32}$ 4) $2\frac{1}{4}$

5) $\frac{3}{8}$ 6) $3\frac{1}{2}$ 7) $\frac{3}{8}$ 8) $\frac{24}{35}$

9) 1 10) 2 11) $\frac{20}{21}$ 12) $3\frac{3}{5}$

13) $\frac{4}{7}$ 14) $1\frac{1}{9}$ 15) 12 16) $\frac{4}{15}$

17) $1\frac{1}{35}$ 18) $\frac{5}{12}$ 19) $1\frac{1}{9}$ 20) $\frac{7}{16}$

21) $\frac{4}{5}$ 22) $5\frac{1}{4}$ 23) $\frac{5}{12}$ 24) $1\frac{2}{5}$

© Libro Studio LLC 2020

Answers

Day 77:
1) $1\frac{1}{2}$ 2) $\frac{5}{14}$ 3) $3\frac{3}{5}$ 4) $1\frac{7}{8}$
5) $\frac{5}{14}$ 6) $\frac{32}{63}$ 7) $2\frac{1}{4}$ 8) $12\frac{3}{5}$
9) $1\frac{2}{3}$ 10) 8 11) $1\frac{1}{9}$ 12) 18
13) $1\frac{1}{5}$ 14) $2\frac{4}{5}$ 15) $\frac{5}{36}$ 16) $\frac{9}{16}$
17) $\frac{3}{10}$ 18) $1\frac{17}{28}$ 19) $\frac{2}{5}$ 20) $1\frac{1}{4}$
21) $1\frac{2}{3}$ 22) $\frac{1}{2}$ 23) $1\frac{7}{8}$ 24) $2\frac{1}{7}$

Day 78:
1) $1\frac{1}{2}$ 2) $1\frac{11}{25}$ 3) $8\frac{4}{7}$ 4) $\frac{3}{7}$
5) $1\frac{11}{16}$ 6) $1\frac{1}{4}$ 7) $\frac{27}{80}$ 8) $\frac{7}{18}$
9) $\frac{6}{7}$ 10) $\frac{1}{3}$ 11) $1\frac{2}{3}$ 12) $\frac{8}{15}$
13) $\frac{8}{21}$ 14) $3\frac{1}{5}$ 15) $\frac{3}{8}$ 16) $2\frac{2}{9}$
17) $4\frac{3}{8}$ 18) $\frac{15}{28}$ 19) $\frac{27}{40}$ 20) $1\frac{1}{3}$
21) $1\frac{1}{9}$ 22) $\frac{1}{4}$ 23) $\frac{7}{9}$ 24) 20

Day 79:
1) $\frac{4}{9}$ 2) $1\frac{7}{8}$ 3) 3 4) $1\frac{3}{5}$
5) $1\frac{13}{14}$ 6) $\frac{9}{64}$ 7) $\frac{7}{16}$ 8) $\frac{3}{5}$
9) $1\frac{1}{2}$ 10) $\frac{9}{10}$ 11) 15 12) $\frac{5}{12}$
13) $1\frac{7}{9}$ 14) $3\frac{5}{9}$ 15) $2\frac{7}{9}$ 16) $1\frac{7}{20}$
17) $\frac{9}{20}$ 18) $3\frac{3}{7}$ 19) 15 20) $1\frac{5}{7}$
21) $1\frac{3}{7}$ 22) $1\frac{1}{2}$ 23) $\frac{4}{9}$ 24) $\frac{15}{28}$

Day 80:
1) 1 2) $\frac{1}{4}$ 3) $\frac{7}{8}$ 4) 6
5) 4 6) $\frac{1}{3}$ 7) $\frac{2}{3}$ 8) $\frac{4}{9}$
9) $1\frac{3}{32}$ 10) 1 11) $2\frac{2}{5}$ 12) $5\frac{1}{3}$
13) $1\frac{5}{7}$ 14) $1\frac{1}{8}$ 15) $1\frac{4}{5}$ 16) $\frac{45}{56}$
17) $\frac{5}{24}$ 18) $1\frac{31}{32}$ 19) $3\frac{1}{3}$ 20) $1\frac{7}{9}$
21) $1\frac{1}{14}$ 22) $\frac{7}{8}$ 23) $1\frac{3}{5}$ 24) $3\frac{3}{5}$

Day 81:
1) 3 2) $1\frac{2}{3}$ 3) $1\frac{3}{4}$ 4) 2
5) $1\frac{9}{16}$ 6) 2 7) 18 8) $1\frac{1}{2}$
9) $10\frac{2}{3}$ 10) $\frac{2}{3}$ 11) $4\frac{2}{3}$ 12) $\frac{1}{8}$
13) $1\frac{2}{25}$ 14) $\frac{9}{10}$ 15) 10 16) $\frac{16}{21}$

Day 82:
1) 10 2) $\frac{3}{4}$ 3) $\frac{7}{12}$ 4) 9
5) $22\frac{1}{2}$ 6) $\frac{16}{35}$ 7) $\frac{4}{5}$ 8) $\frac{2}{7}$
9) $2\frac{1}{2}$ 10) $\frac{16}{21}$ 11) $\frac{1}{6}$ 12) $\frac{20}{63}$
13) $\frac{8}{9}$ 14) $1\frac{1}{2}$ 15) $2\frac{4}{7}$ 16) $\frac{5}{12}$
17) $\frac{9}{14}$ 18) $\frac{8}{9}$ 19) 5 20) $1\frac{7}{9}$
21) $\frac{1}{3}$ 22) $\frac{3}{28}$ 23) $\frac{35}{72}$ 24) $1\frac{13}{35}$

Day 83:
1) $\frac{2}{5}$ 2) $2\frac{6}{7}$ 3) 4 4) $\frac{10}{27}$
5) $1\frac{1}{2}$ 6) $3\frac{1}{5}$ 7) 9 8) $\frac{1}{4}$
9) $\frac{5}{6}$ 10) $\frac{25}{28}$ 11) $16\frac{2}{3}$ 12) $\frac{1}{27}$
13) 9 14) 6 15) 15 16) $\frac{1}{3}$
17) $\frac{16}{27}$ 18) $1\frac{5}{27}$ 19) $\frac{3}{4}$ 20) 4
21) $1\frac{2}{3}$ 22) $1\frac{2}{5}$ 23) $7\frac{1}{5}$ 24) $5\frac{5}{8}$

Day 84:
1) $2\frac{4}{5}$ 2) $1\frac{7}{9}$ 3) $\frac{2}{3}$ 4) $2\frac{1}{4}$
5) 4 6) $\frac{9}{16}$ 7) $\frac{2}{5}$ 8) $\frac{7}{8}$
9) $3\frac{1}{2}$ 10) 18 11) $9\frac{1}{3}$ 12) $\frac{1}{6}$
13) $\frac{4}{5}$ 14) $5\frac{2}{5}$ 15) 5 16) $\frac{1}{4}$
17) 12 18) $6\frac{3}{4}$ 19) $3\frac{1}{3}$ 20) $1\frac{1}{3}$
21) $1\frac{2}{3}$ 22) $1\frac{11}{16}$ 23) $\frac{10}{21}$ 24) $2\frac{1}{12}$

Day 85:
1) $3\frac{3}{4}$ 2) $\frac{4}{9}$ 3) 7 4) $1\frac{1}{4}$
5) 5 6) $11\frac{2}{3}$ 7) $\frac{7}{12}$ 8) $\frac{8}{9}$
9) 10 10) $2\frac{1}{2}$ 11) $4\frac{1}{2}$ 12) 1
13) $1\frac{7}{8}$ 14) $2\frac{1}{4}$ 15) $3\frac{3}{4}$ 16) $\frac{5}{12}$
17) $1\frac{1}{3}$ 18) $\frac{4}{9}$ 19) $\frac{4}{35}$ 20) $7\frac{1}{2}$
21) $\frac{18}{85}$ 22) $\frac{4}{15}$ 23) $2\frac{1}{2}$ 24) $\frac{8}{9}$

Day 86:
1) 5 2) $\frac{5}{9}$ 3) 5 4) $2\frac{1}{2}$
5) $\frac{5}{8}$ 6) 2 7) 24 8) $\frac{7}{8}$
9) $3\frac{3}{7}$ 10) $1\frac{1}{2}$ 11) $7\frac{1}{2}$ 12) $\frac{1}{3}$
13) 12 14) $\frac{10}{49}$ 15) 24 16) $\frac{18}{35}$
17) $2\frac{26}{27}$ 18) $1\frac{7}{8}$ 19) $\frac{3}{5}$ 20) 3
21) $3\frac{3}{8}$ 22) $\frac{8}{9}$ 23) $1\frac{1}{2}$ 24) 18

Day 87:
1) $\frac{5}{24}$ 2) $\frac{9}{40}$ 3) $\frac{2}{9}$ 4) $\frac{7}{12}$
5) $\frac{3}{10}$ 6) 6 7) 24 8) $2\frac{5}{8}$
9) $\frac{3}{32}$ 10) $1\frac{13}{14}$ 11) $10\frac{1}{2}$ 12) $9\frac{1}{3}$
13) 16 14) $\frac{3}{4}$ 15) 5 16) $1\frac{1}{4}$
17) $5\frac{1}{3}$ 18) $7\frac{1}{2}$ 19) $2\frac{1}{2}$ 20) $3\frac{1}{2}$
21) 12 22) $2\frac{2}{3}$ 23) $11\frac{2}{3}$ 24) $\frac{7}{15}$

Day 88:
1) $\frac{5}{6}$ 2) $2\frac{6}{7}$ 3) 12 4) $\frac{1}{8}$
5) $5\frac{1}{4}$ 6) $\frac{8}{27}$ 7) $3\frac{3}{7}$ 8) 1
9) $\frac{15}{28}$ 10) $\frac{9}{20}$ 11) $1\frac{7}{9}$ 12) $1\frac{13}{32}$
13) 28 14) $4\frac{1}{2}$ 15) $7\frac{1}{9}$ 16) $\frac{2}{3}$
17) $2\frac{6}{7}$ 18) $\frac{4}{9}$ 19) $6\frac{2}{5}$ 20) $4\frac{1}{2}$
21) $\frac{5}{16}$ 22) $1\frac{1}{4}$ 23) $7\frac{1}{2}$ 24) $\frac{7}{18}$

© Libro Studio LLC 2020

Answers

Day 89:

1) $3\frac{1}{3}$ 2) $4\frac{1}{6}$ 3) $\frac{1}{14}$ 4) $\frac{3}{4}$

5) $\frac{1}{5}$ 6) $8\frac{1}{3}$ 7) $5\frac{1}{16}$ 8) $\frac{7}{18}$

9) $\frac{1}{5}$ 10) $\frac{9}{14}$ 11) $\frac{3}{5}$ 12) $\frac{1}{9}$

13) $8\frac{1}{3}$ 14) $6\frac{3}{7}$ 15) $\frac{2}{3}$ 16) $\frac{9}{10}$

17) $3\frac{1}{3}$ 18) $\frac{5}{14}$ 19) $1\frac{1}{5}$ 20) $1\frac{1}{3}$

21) $\frac{20}{21}$ 22) 2 23) $2\frac{1}{7}$ 24) $\frac{2}{3}$

Day 90:

1) $2\frac{1}{2}$ 2) $4\frac{1}{2}$ 3) $\frac{4}{7}$ 4) 36

5) $11\frac{1}{4}$ 6) $1\frac{5}{27}$ 7) 1 8) $\frac{9}{20}$

9) $\frac{3}{10}$ 10) $1\frac{1}{3}$ 11) $\frac{1}{10}$ 12) $4\frac{1}{2}$

13) $2\frac{4}{5}$ 14) $6\frac{3}{4}$ 15) $\frac{3}{5}$ 16) $\frac{4}{5}$

17) $\frac{1}{2}$ 18) $10\frac{2}{7}$ 19) $2\frac{5}{8}$ 20) $\frac{1}{6}$

21) $1\frac{5}{9}$ 22) 20 23) $\frac{3}{5}$ 24) $1\frac{1}{4}$

Day 91:

1) 17 points 2) 94% 3) 125 trees 4) 84%

Day 92:

1) 42 hits 2) 8% 3) 10.80 dollars 4) 1,500 seats

Day 93:

1) 14% 2) 65.38 gigabytes 3) 64% 4) $\frac{1}{2}$

Day 94:

1) 120 dollars 2) 63.75 dollars 3) 31.80 dollars
4) 21.22 dollars

Day 95:

1) 600 doughnuts 2) 60% 3) 120 doughnuts
4) 160%

Day 96:

1) 60 dollars 2) 300 dollars 3) 500 dollars
4) 135 dollars

Day 97:

1) 112 votes 2) 140 votes 3) 148 votes 4) 9 votes

Day 98:

1) 8 pizzas 2) 36 dollars 3) 1.25 dollars 4) 6 pizzas

Day 99:

1) 76% 2) 252 bullseyes 3) 100% 4) 21 arrows

Day 100:

1) 5,000 gold coins 2) 325 gold coins 3) 9 stories
4) 700 guests

© 2020, Libro Studio LLC. The purchase of this publication entitles the buyer to reproduce pages for classroom use only—not for commercial resale. Reproduction of this publication's material for an entire school or district is prohibited. No part of this book may be reproduced (except as noted above), transmitted in any form or by any means, electronic or mechanical, including photocopying, recording, or any other information storage and retrieval system, without the written permission of the publisher.

ISBN: 978-1-63578-318-6

Current contact information for Libro Studio LLC can be found at
www.HumbleMath.com
www.LibroStudioLLC.com

Disclaimers:

The creator and publisher DO NOT GUARANTEE THE ACCURACY, RELIABILITY, OR COMPLETENESS OF THE CONTENT OF THIS BOOK OR RELATED RESOURSES AND IS NOT RESPONSIBLE FOR ANY ERRORS OR OMISSIONS. We apologize for any inaccurate, outdated, or misleading information. Feel free to contact us if you have questions or concerns.

Information in this book should not be considered advice nor treated as advice. ALWAYS SEEK ADVICE FROM A QUALIFIED PROFESSIONAL BEFORE MAKING DECISIONS BASED ON THE INFORMATION FOUND IN THIS BOOK OR RELATED RESOURCES. The creator and publisher are not liable for any decision made or action taken based on this book's content and information nor that of any related resource. You and any other persons are responsible for your own judgments, decisions, and actions.

Other resources, such as, but not limited to websites, videos, individuals, and organizations, may be referenced in this book or related resources but THIS DOES NOT MEAN THE CREATOR OR PUBLISHER ENDORSES THE INFORMATION THAT IS PROVIDED BY THESE RESOURCES. The creator and publisher of this book will not be liable for any information, claim, or recommendation obtained from these referenced resources. These referenced resources may also become outdated or unavailable. Websites, links, videos, and other resources may be changed, altered or removed over time.

This book and its contents are provided "AS IS" without warranty of any kind, expressed or implied, and hereby disclaims all implied warranties, including any warranty of merchantability and warranty of fitness for a particular purpose.

Libro Studio LLC publishes books and other content in a variety of print and electronic formats. Some content that appears in one format may not be available in other formats. For example, some content found in a print book may not be available in the eBook format, and vice versa. Furthermore, Libro Studio LLC reserves the right to update, alter, unpublish, and/or republish the content of any of these formats at any time.

Made in the USA
Monee, IL
12 May 2022

96266542R10059